# A LONG WAY BACK:

## Education in Sierra Leone

By Dr. Christopher J. Gardner

**Setting up a GenHybrid Learning System in Kamakwie**

innovativeink PUBLISHING

A Division of Kendall Hunt

Cover design & illustration by Chris Gardner.

www.innovativeinkpublishing.com
*Send all inquiries to:*
4050 Westmark Drive
Dubuque, IA  52004-1840

# Contents

# Acknowledgments

This book has found its place in the world of nonfiction as my GenHybrid Systems learning endeavors in Sierra Leone drew to a close. I wanted to thank everybody at Develop Africa for their continued support and guidance. Many thanks go out to the Wesleyan Secondary School principals, their pastor Daniel, and my social media team without whose support our Sierra Leone education venture might never have seen the light of day.

At this point in time, I also wanted to let my family—Ray, Mia, and Dawn—know how much their never-ending belief in this project meant to me. I am hopeful that with their continued love and support, I will be able to deliver many more education-related books in the years to come.

Last but not least, I wanted to take a moment to give a shout-out to all the Salonians who I have met along the way, and who have helped shape this memorable story. Keep up the faith and good work in protecting your freedom and democracy. We are rooting for you!

# 1

# Sierra Leone as an Idea for Improved Learning

In early November of 2021, the morning of my upcoming flight to Free-town, Sierra Leone, I was still roaming around the office trying to gather all the essentials needed to make this a successful journey. My imminent expedition was to a faraway country in West Africa that I had first learned about from my college liberal arts classes and again a few years later when watching the movie, *Blood Diamond*. I still remembered my sociology professor discussing world genocides and acknowledging that the Sierra Leonean Civil War as an extreme case of genocide. Maybe this is where my interest all began.

My interest in the country and their courageous people was awakened. The Civil War that lasted from March 23, 1991 to January 11, 2002, had taken its toll. Around 200,000 people lost their lives, and another 2 million people lost their homes. The entire nation was devastated over an 11-year period, a testimony to what a corrupt regime can do to its own people.

Before the outbreak of the war, Sierra Leone had a longstanding history of Western-style education. In the mid-19th century, the country had served as the most important training center for doctors, administrators, and educators all throughout West Africa. Fast forward to the 20th century and Sierra Leone was facing an unprecedented learning crisis in which only 8% of third graders could independently read. On the other hand, the most educated person in the world was born and raised in Freetown, Sierra Leone. His name is Dr. Abdul Karim Bangura. He holds five PhDs and speaks 18 languages fluently, helping him become the President and Ambassador to the United Nations of the Association of Third World Studies (ATWS).

This contradiction gave me an indication that the deep-rooted Sierra Leonean belief in the value of education just needed to be reawakened and infused with new ideas. Dr. Bangura once said in an interview with the *Sierra Express Media* that the current situation could also be "an opportunity to go and help tear down and rebuild the educational system from the ground up." Possibly a new way to deliver information that would work better with existing infrastructure could offer a fresh start.

Ever since the beginning of my doctoral studies in 2012, I had become obsessed with the idea of hybrid learning systems and their advantages within education. My preliminary research led to an initial proposal that outlined a social hybrid education learning system to improve cross-cultural understanding. The proposal was shut down by my dissertation Chair and Committee Members since there "hadn't been such a thing done in the past, and therefore it couldn't be measured."

By the end of my doctoral studies, the finalized dissertation revolved around mobile gaming and its effects on business within technology. Nevertheless, I was determined to revive my original idea and to put it to the test. Sierra Leone seemed the perfect fit and ready for a change.

At the time, hybrid learning, or as it was referred to, "blended learning," had not yet been practiced across geographic regions. My idea was to create an intercultural experience to improve education so young learners could gain new insights from each other. The overarching idea was to let young minds take control to explore newfound possibilities by giving them an online platform that would allow for creative learning and growth.

My research led me down a new path: the introduction of an innovative hybrid learning educational system in the Sierra Leone, from Grades K through 12. It quickly became apparent that most Sierra Leoneans who resided in Freetown's upscale neighborhoods had access to a privileged education. Their schools were largely private and, thus, were permitted to establish their own curricula (16.2%). Underdeveloped Freetown areas, the outskirts, or most other parts of the country did not have the resources or infrastructure in place to offer a decent primary or secondary education. Those districts relied heavily on government funding and general assistance (70%).

The idea that this small West African country had such a rich and diverse history of education convinced me to contact people there to be an advocate for change. My research led me to a small group called "Develop Africa," whose focus was predominantly on Sierra Leone and education. I learned that the organization was based in Nashville, TN, but also had local offices in Freetown, Sierra Leone.

Sylvester became my point of contact. We started meeting online via Zoom. I started by explaining my ideas for hybrid learning and how I had become an advocate for change in education. Sylvester was receptive to my ideas and very forthcoming. He let me know that Sierra Leone was in desperate need of change and that education could serve as a catapult. These initial meetings served as the beginning of a great journey.

Shortly after getting acquainted with Sylvester, I decided to start putting together a team in charge of an online presence to make people aware of the upcoming initiative. Putting a working team together took more time than anticipated, and it all started with brand development.

Part of team planning is the "big picture" thinking. We decided that putting together a working computer lab as a starting point for the hybrid learning system was a priority in an underdeveloped West African country such as Sierra Leone. This required not only the necessary equipment but also the installation of a curriculum for students to engage with and the hiring of qualified teachers to instruct students unaccustomed to a regular school schedule for large parts of their education.

Thinking about those possible outcomes was overwhelming to say the least. I had to take a step back and remind myself that it might be best to just take it a day at a time. It became obvious that I needed to bring the initiative to the public first, before engaging partners in Sierra Leone.

The idea of GenHybrid Systems, LLC, was born. I started initiating contact with social media experts and some of my former students to help with online marketing efforts. We started putting together a website (www.genhybridsystems.com) that would serve as an information platform and created Facebook, Instagram, YouTube, and TikTok accounts to inform people about the upcoming initiative.

Partnering up with Develop Africa became a key component in our strategy. Sylvester was very keen on providing insights into the culture in Sierra Leone. When deciding on what region to focus our efforts in, Sylvester pointed out that his project manager Abu, who was based out of Freetown, had a longstanding connection to the Wesleyan School. Wesleyan Secondary is a K-12 school based in Kamakwie and its surrounding villages. The school gave students the opportunity to graduate from high school and to move on to postsecondary education. This town was in the Northwest Province of Sierra Leone.

The journey I was about to embark on was one that would change my life forever. But first thing's first: Planning the trip alongside the upcoming media campaign was not an easy task. It was 2021, and COVID-19 had become a worldwide pandemic. Planning a trip to West Africa was always going to include Malaria and Ebola shots, but now the pandemic meant an additional vaccination and certification as proof for a visa application to enter the country. As it turned out, the process required me to get a small booklet that had all my vaccinations listed and stamped as part of the entry requirements of the Sierra Leonean government.

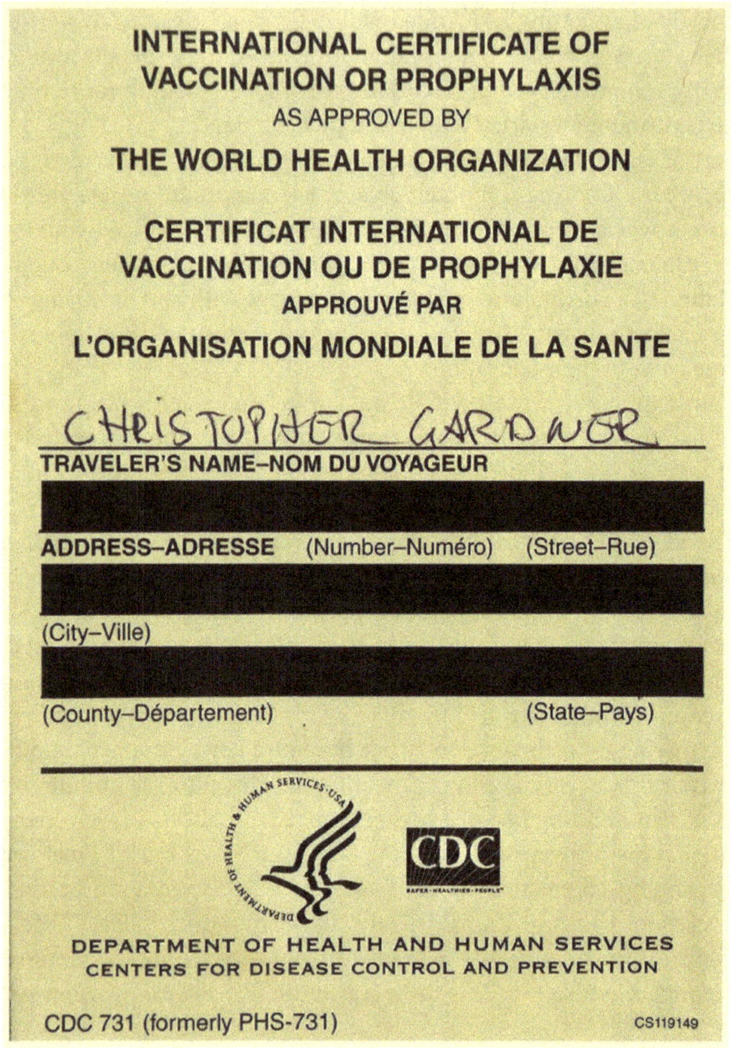


*International Certificate of Vaccination required before entering Sierra Leone*

I was never a big fan of needles. "Surely, this was going to be the worst of it," I kept on telling myself. I just had to get past a little bodily inconvenience and things were going to look up. The excitement of travelling into the unknown and seeing my adventure unfold was starting to sink in. I had to keep on reminding myself to stay focused.

The website to promote the undertaking of building a computer lab and classroom space as an addition to an already existing school was well underway. At the same time, we sketched out ideas for a logo that was going to be the centerpiece of our brand. Shortly after that we started publishing on social media to notify the community about the upcoming enterprise. It was an exciting time for everyone involved. We had a couple of outside studios working on content creation and video editing, a separate content manager, a web developer, and another designer (besides me) art-directing the entire project.

There was a strong sense of urgency. Under a tight deadline, all media content needed to go live as soon as possible. The plan was to keep on publishing and uploading new material that I was going to provide once I had boots on the ground. As it turned out, getting to Freetown was quite an undertaking.

After I had finally gathered all the equipment and paperwork required for this trip and was at the airport, it occurred to me that I was going to be traveling for a long time. But not in my wildest dreams could I have imagined how long.

My 9:00 a.m. flight from Las Vegas to Newark was straightforward. When I had lived in the Northeastern part of the United States, I had flown in and out of Newark on numerous occasions. I arrived in Newark at 4:50 p.m. My layover was nearly 3 hours, so I decided to get a good meal. My connecting flight was going to arrive in Brussels the following day at 7:45 a.m., so it made sense for me to get a hot lunch before embarking on that long stretch across the Atlantic Ocean. Sitting at one of the terminal's finer dining establishments, I felt a strange tightness developing in my lower back. After a little bewilderment, I placed my order and chalked it up to stiffness and travel stress.

The burger came out medium-rare and was served with a side of fries. It all went down easily with a large glass of ice-cold Stella. Very fitting I thought, since my layover was in Brussels. Belgian beer had been my favorite for a long time. Although I am a native German, and we do have great variety of fantastic beers in Germany, there was always something I liked better about Belgian beer. Even in my younger years I enjoyed a Belgian blond over a Hefeweizen. (Although, a couple of pints of Hefeweizen amongst friends was always a good excuse to get out of the house.)

As I was sitting at my table, reminiscing about the "good ol' days," the waitress brought my check, and I noticed that boarding was about to start.

Once I boarded the plane and was finally in my seat, a feeling of excitement or "butterflies in my stomach" started to take hold. It was as though the fact that this project was happening suddenly became real to me.

I was on my way to an unknown-to-me West African country to meet people I had never met in person to build an educational facility. My desire to foster new educational opportunities in an underdeveloped educational system that had been broken for a long time was becoming a reality. I was on my way to Brussels en route to Freetown, Sierra Leone!

# 2

# Making Landfall in Freetown

After arriving at the airport in Brussels, I decided to walk directly to my connecting gate, not yet anticipating the added security stations for travelers. COVID-19-card inspections were also in place at McCarran Airport in Las Vegas, but now that I had arrived in Brussels, it seemed that monitoring stations and checkpoints had been set up in every terminal. My projected 10-minute walk turned into a 2-hour ordeal. Luckily my layover was close to 3 hours. The last thing I wanted was to get stuck somewhere along the way.

As I was standing in line to get my temperature taken and paperwork reviewed by one of the control agents, I again noticed a slow but steady pain in my lower back. I could not recall having had any kind of back problems before, so this was a new and very untimely sensation. The pain was getting more severe with every passing minute, and I felt as though something was telling me to turn around and abort my mission. The discomfort forced me to take a seat on my backpack, using it as a chair, as I was standing in a long line, mostly Africans trying to get home.

As I was sitting on my makeshift chair, an older lady in traditional African attire approached me. "Have you been to Sierra Leone before?" she asked.

At this point, the pain in my back had gotten worse, and I started to shift around in hopes of finding some kind of relief.

"No, this is my first trip to West Africa, but I have been in Morocco before," I responded.

Her eyes started searching my face.

"Are you feeling unwell?" she asked with genuine concern in her voice. "To be honest with you, I'm experiencing some pain in my lower back, but I couldn't tell you why," I said.

A slight smile that gave me hope broadened across her face at once. "Oh, have you started taking Malaria medication recently?" Again, her confident voice made me realize that she had a good idea what the culprit of my discomfort was. I was quick to let her know that I had indeed started taking my Malaria medication only a few days prior to my departure, as was recommended by my physician.

"Yes, he should have also explained to you that in case of discomfort Ibuprofen will neutralize the pain," she continued.

"Oh, one of the blogs had recommended to take along a bottle of children's Ibuprofen," I recalled.

With lightning speed, I opened the laces on my backpack and rummaged through my toiletry bag. At once I found that little grape-flavored remedy and decided to take two pills instead of just one. The pain started to subside as quickly as it came. Within 10 minutes I as able to freely walk around again and carry on my conversation with the mysterious "healer" that might have saved my trip before it even started.

"You are truly a godsend. Without your help I might have abandoned my journey altogether. I was seriously considering leaving the airport to try to find a nearby hospital. Honestly, the pain was starting to worry me quite a bit, and I never go to the doctor. Now come to think of it, I have only been to the hospital twice in my life. Once when I was a little kid, and then because of an unfortunate incident in my college days." I did not feel like elaborating and offered a big smile instead.

"Well, some things are just meant to be. Of course, it is also common knowledge that Malaria medication will affect the lower lumbar region of the spine." At once she burst into tears laughing all the while patting my back. Strangely enough her amusement gave me comfort.

Once all ailments had subsided and my positive outlook was restored, I was overcome by a feeling of strength. Maybe it was just the positive influence of my new friend or the fact that I was pain free again, but either way I had a newfound sense of inspiration and was able to get some much-needed rest on my connecting flight to Freetown, Sierra Leone.

Once we were about to descend, I woke up to a bright red-orange sun slowly setting on the ocean, offering a lovely reflection on the water and serving as a gateway into this mysterious metropolis.

Freetown was founded by Granville Sharp, a British abolitionist, in 1787. It was the biggest port town in Sierra Leone and had served as a hub for freed slaves since the early 1700s. In 1961, the country had finally gained its independence from the United Kingdom but remained a hotbed of turmoil.

As the plane was making landfall, I had forgotten about all my research and data from the last couple of months. The breathtaking sunset and ease of the plane gliding onto the runway made for an unexpected welcome indeed. I was still buzzing from the comfort of my chair, when my fellow passengers abruptly started moving toward the exit doors, as the announcement of mandatory COVID-19 testing was announced.

If at this point, I had developed any kind of romantic notion about this West African country, I was in for a rude awakening. Exiting the plane, I quickly realized that the starry-eyed, honeymoon phase would be short-lived. Instead, the everyday grind of our "relationship" was about to be jump-started. Finding myself the only white person standing in the middle of a terminal, surrounded by a sea of Sierra Leoneans and other Africans, was a sobering experience. As I stood there dumbfounded, activity, constant movement, unfamiliar sounding dialects, and other noises all around me, my natural instincts seemed to be taking control of my body, and I started moving in the general direction of the baggage claim area.

But nothing and nobody could have prepared me for what I was about to witness inside the building where the carousels were located. It felt as though I had been transported into one of those sci-fi movies, where the world is coming to an end and everybody is trying to leave town all at once. The carousels were spinning, stacked high with luggage. Ten- to twelve-feet high piles of bags were scattered alongside the walls. In this mayhem were hundreds of people trying to secure their belongings, while security guards armed with automatic weapons walked through the masses scanning the premises for "suspicious activity."

It was truly a site to see. For the first time in my life was I stunned to the point where I had to take a seat. Naturally, I was thinking that I might never find my bag in all this turmoil, and the thought of getting some helpful information left my mind again as soon as it had entered. Without much hope, but knowing that I had to keep on moving, I got up and walked toward the carousel displaying my flight number. Lo and behold, my bag was standing upright on the conveyor belt coming my way just as I approached the scene.

It felt as though I had just won the lottery. Without wasting any more precious time, I bolted toward my bag, all the while bumping into people. I forcefully yanked it off the transporter and started heading toward the sliding doors when I was approached by an airport official.

"Did you get your entry papers stamped already, Sir?" I could hear him ask me in what I could have guessed was the English-based creole language called Krio.

"Well, no. I didn't realize that I had to," was my response.

"But of course you must, Dear Sir. Please come with me. I can get you ahead of the line if you wish."

With those words the polite official urged me to follow him. We started moving quickly through the crowd as he parted the way for me. Finally, I was leaving the insanely busy terminal. I felt a sudden relief that was, again, unfortunately very short-lived. My guide went to open a door that had a plaque sign placed over it that read, "Office," and another handwritten piece of paper pasted up with masking tape to the side of the door that read, "For Official COVID Testing."

Inside the "office" I was greeted by rows of chairs that were populated with anxious-looking travelers. I had to make my peace with the idea that I was going to stay here at the airport for a long time. The question simply was how to move forward in the queue.

"Oh, you will get tested here for COVID. But don't worry, I will get your name on the list, so you don't have to wait."

With that the man gave me a very large grin. Somehow, this stranger made me feel like this was the most normal thing in the world. "You just have to sign-in here, Dear Sir." With that he pointed out a crumpled-up piece of paper that was placed on what appeared to be a patio table.

"Don't mind the time slot there. I will get you to the front of the line," he said, and urged me to follow him to another, more official looking desk that was manned by another man in an airport uniform. My tour guide initiated a brief conversation in Krio with the man behind the desk. Then he gave me another one of those winning smiles and said, "Dear Sir, this gentleman will take care of you now. Please take a seat over here."

I took my seat in the front row and had only two people ahead of me in the queue. After another little discussion with the man behind the desk, my guide returned to stand in front of me and let me know that a little help aiding his family would be appreciated.

"Anything helps, Dear Sir," he said, while keeping his outstretched palm hidden from the public eye. I was very appreciative of his help in guiding me through the maze of lines that started forming everywhere. In retrospect, it was very also very helpful of the Develop Africa people to let me know to always carry a few one-dollar bills in my pocket. "This will come in very handy once you make landfall in Freetown," they said during one of our long Zoom calls.

Sitting in front of another makeshift table, as a nurse was starting to take my temperature, my mind started wandering again. I saw people's happy faces on my virtual call screen and heard their loud laughter and lighthearted exchanges of inside jokes that put me into a positive state of mind. Yes, I was exhausted, and I was in desperate need of a hot shower and some rest, but who would have guessed that those prep sessions were going to help me one day in the not-so-distant future?

Those memories put a faint smile on my tired face and gave me a sudden burst of energy. As soon as I was finally allowed to leave the airport, I pulled out my phone to greet the world, ready to embark on my much-anticipated adventure. Unfortunately, one of the many soldiers stationed outside of the airport approached me with one outstretched hand, cautioning me while I glanced at his other hand firmly that was pressed to an automatic weapon.

"You are not allowed to take videos or pictures on the airport premises," he said as he swiftly walked up to my side. I finished my video but made sure to complete my sentence and to get him into my last frame before sending off the video.

"Sorry for that," I said as I walked toward the taxi area.

Getting to the city center was a little tricky. This was another thing Develop Africa had cautioned me about: "Make sure to call the ferry people beforehand and schedule an appointment for them to pick you up with their shuttle bus from the airport. It is very important to do that before you board your plane to Sierra Leone. They do not commute every day, and you don't want to get stranded."

Contrary to this, I felt as though I needed to prove them wrong by leaving "cold turkey." In hindsight, being chauffeured to the marina and leaving all that airport madness behind, I felt as though this may have been the best decision that I ever made.

The shuttle went through a lot of deserted neighborhoods. We had to conquer some rough patches, and at one time I felt as though we might be off-roading. By the time we finally arrived at the docks, it was well past midnight. Communicating with the local people was not that challenging. They had their own accent but understood me very well. Naturally, it was going to take some time before I sounded like a local, though.

# 3

# First Discoveries

The people working at the dock were very hospitable and offered me my first Star Lager beer, while I was waiting on my ferry to arrive. I hadn't slept in a long time, but my adventure had begun, and I was eager to see new faces and make new acquaintances. I learned that Star Lager was really the only beer offered in a lot of places here. My German heritage made the taste a little shocking at first. As it turned out, though, the beer grew on me. Another alcoholic beverage I learned to enjoy was "poyo." It is the local hooch made from the sap collected from a variety of palm trees, but more about that later.

The boat ride into the city harbor was very quick. Most passengers went below deck to find their seat and to take a quick nap. I decided to stay on the upper deck instead. The stiff breeze made it a challenge to hold on to the railing, but it was worth the effort. Soon after departing, I was able to see the city lights in the distance. As we got closer, the glow of the lights got more intense, and the cityscape was unfolding before me. What a marvelous way to be introduced to Freetown!

Luckily, I had already arranged for a taxi to pick me up from the port. The cab ride from the harbor to the city was another scenic trip. I had booked my hotel room way in advance, which turned out to be a good idea. After such a long and intense journey, all my preparations had been necessary, even though I'm not normally a big planner.

The hotel had all the crucial comforts after a long trip. The room had working AC and a backyard pool for soaking. My goal was not to get too comfortable because the real adventure was about to begin, but I was in desperate need of some rest. After a good night's sleep, I ate an outstanding breakfast that consisted of different types of fruit, eggs benedict, and a variety of meats and toast. The coffee was fresh, and the atmosphere at the hotel was upbeat. I couldn't have asked for a better place to refuel and get prepared for the task at hand.

The very next day I started exploring the neighborhood. Although the hotel was very pleasant and, even by Western standards, well-equipped, the surrounding area reminded me why I had come here in the first place. I had started my day early in hopes of discovering as much as possible; hence, I was armed with my Canon Rebel T8 and ready to shoot some video to be uploaded onto Google Drive for my team to turn into meaningful social media posts.

As soon as I had left the premises, it became apparent to me that it might not be such a good idea to flaunt my bright red, expensive camera in public for everyone to see. At the same time, I needed to get usable footage to document my stay in Sierra Leone. So, I detached the video stick to make the camera a little less flashy. It gave me freer range and lightened my movement. Of course, I was also able to disguise my camera a little better this way as well.

What a first day it turned out to be! I made friends with an older couple who were getting chicken from a street vendor, a military security guard stationed on the sidewalk of one of the major streets, and some other local folks who were just curious about me and what I was up to. I never had the feeling that the locals had any ill intentions toward me. It was more a mutual curiosity that had brought us together. I wanted to know more about their culture and way of life, whereas they seemed to just be interested in me as a person.

Some of the side streets were very isolated, except for some stray dogs that were running in packs. Every now and then I came across someone sitting by the side of a collapsed house or leaning on one of the many dilapidated walls that were part of the urban landscape, subtle reminders of the Civil War that had ravaged the country not so many years ago. It felt as though Sierra Leoneans still hadn't made peace with the atrocities and crimes against humanity committed during those dreadful years of agony and despair. The urban decay testified to that chapter in Sierra Leonean history. Although the city's inhabitants seemed upbeat, the atmosphere was a reminder of what once was, but never again could or would be.

The second day I decided to start out early, knowing that Abu, the Develop Africa representative, was going to catch up with me later that day. I was eager to get out and taste a local cup of coffee. Unfortunately, I was once again confronted with the outcomes of the Civil War that had negatively impacted local farmers and their coffee plantations.

After a little while my search led me to a local coffee shop on the corner of a buzzing intersection. A police man, who was standing in the middle of this pandemonium trying to navigate traffic, gave me an inpatient look as I jaywalked right under his nose.

*During the height of the COVID-19 pandemic security guards*
*wore masks even outdoors*

*The buzzing city of Freetown and its traffic control*

The coffee shop had an old sign that read "Coffee Shoppe," and the owner had seen me coming a mile away. With a broad smile on his face, he said, "Don't worry about the police. They really have nothing to say. Here, in Freetown, you are truly free." He burst out laughing but quieted down again quickly. "We tolerate them but don't pay them any mind," he said, letting out another loud and contagious laugh.

He introduced himself as Daniel as he turned and walked behind the counter to brew me a fresh cup of coffee. As he worked, he turned to face me.

"Now, the military men you see here in their grey uniforms are an entirely different story. Don't mess with them. They are no joke and have nobody to answer to," he said with a serous face.

I got the message and felt like I had been warned. The coffee was served in an oversized, hand-painted mug, and the strong, rich flavor made me wonder aloud about why there weren't more coffee shops around. Daniel was happy to fill me in.

"Well, you see, I was here during that awful time. Yes, I was exactly here where I'm standing now. This place had been around for over 50 years. My father and his brother had bought this little corner building in 1970 and turned the first floor into a thriving creole restaurant where coffee was served with every meal. Then came this awful war. You know about our Civil War that lasted from 1991 to 2002?" Without waiting for an answer, he continued, "That conflict created a lot of instability in our country and destroyed most of our agricultural exports. Before the war, our coffee plants were much in demand. Now there is just no financing available. The government has forgotten about us altogether. At times it really feels as though we are left on our own." Intently looking at me, he took a long pause, "Now what brings you to our neck of the woods, My Dear Sir?"

I was still trying to take in all the information that was given to me so freely: "Well, to make a long story short, I flew in from the U.S. to start an education project alongside an organization that has offices here in Freetown."

Daniel's face lit up with pure joy this time: "That is fantastic. We need real education here. You know, after the war our youth was lost. Most of the schools were shattered or burned out because the guerilla fighters used them as strongholds. Starting something here should be considered a blessing for our country."

I'm not sure why it came as a surprise to me, but somehow it caught me off-guard how this man was so in touch with what mattered most.

"You know, I just flew close to 7,000 miles and endless hours to meet with some officials that know the 'in's-and-out's' of your education system, but instead I should just stay here and talk to you a little while longer," I told him.

His eyes opened wide, and he seemed to gasp for air. He grabbed my shoulder and said in a loud, celebratory voice, "You flew almost 7,000 miles to get here? Couldn't you have saved yourself the trouble and done a Zoom call?"

As I was walking back to my hotel several people approached me to strike up random conversations and to inquire about my whereabouts. Although I was still jetlagged, the locals' positive energy was inspiring. I felt welcomed and a genuine appreciation for my arrival. Many people that day learned about my project, some on the walk back to my hotel. Of course, it was apparent that some of bystanders were eager to learn about possible job opportunities; however, for the most part, people were just glad that somebody was trying to do something.

As soon as I entered the hotel lobby, the front desk person approached me: "You have a guest waiting for you. I sent him to the dining area. Were you waiting for somebody today?"

It had been a long morning, but I was eager to get started. As I entered the parlor, I saw only one person who was sitting at the end of a long table.

He smiled when I called out, "Hey, Abu, it is great to meet you finally in person." We had met before on lengthy video conferences, but now I was able to finally make a meaningful connection with my new liaison.

"Yes, indeed. It is so good to finally meet you. How was your long flight?" His English was impeccable, as I had already noticed during our Zoom meetings, but in person he almost sounded like he had an American accent. The people I had encountered at the airport and in the city spoke in the Krio dialect. It was stronger than the Louisiana Cajun or Creole I had encountered in the past and would take me a couple of weeks to adjust to. But I felt motivated and was very hopeful that I could pick up on the native tongue sometime soon.

"My trip was about 27 hours long, but what matters is that I am here now. What are our plans for today?" I asked in eager anticipation.

"I was thinking that we could just start by going to the Develop Africa office and introducing you to everyone," Abu said.

As we were driving through the city of Freetown I was not only introduced to the hustling and bustling, vibrant city, but also to its positive energy.

*First impressions driving through Freetown, Sierra Leone*

Once we arrived at the local Develop Africa office, Abu started introducing me to the staff. Some of them were attending a seminar that I was able to sit in on. The instructions were very focused, and engagement was exceptional. The amount of information that the speakers shared within a very short period was a bit overwhelming. The technology used, equipment, and office space here, none were up to Western standards. But what the organization was lacking in equipment and setting, they made up for it in knowledge and tenacity.

*Develop Africa staff seminar in session*

At the end of the day, we agreed that it would be best to head toward Kamakwie as soon as possible. It was already late April, and the heavy monsoon rainfall was expected to hit our area any day now. Traditionally, the wet season started in early- to mid-May. The roads leading from coastal Freetown toward Kamakwie were going to be un-drivable. Abu explained that mud slides have been a problem during the rainy season for the last few years, mostly due to deforestation.

During our drive, I learned that this beautiful West African country had lost almost 40% of its lush forest since the early 2000s. Due to the ongoing deforestation and land grab, the national forest's clean water reserves had come under scrutiny. The investigation showed that the state-owned Guma Water Company had reported alarming water shortages in the foreseeable future. Other consequences of deforestation included landslides, soil erosion, and the loss of species that had called those forests their home for many centuries.

The most vulnerable species under threat was the chimpanzee; only 5,500 remained as of 2024. Later, during our National Forest trip, I learned it wasn't just the wild western chimpanzees that were endangered. Hippos, baboons, forest buffalos, and African leopards were also endangered. Apparently at one point elephants could be seen grazing the land. Unfortunately, I couldn't see such amazing sights. My new colleagues explained to me how the majestic beauty of those large animals and their presence was felt by the people and seemed to elevate life.

*Deforestation and its devastating effects on animal species and mankind*

The majority of our drive to Kamakwie was off road. Living in the desert for many years, I hadn't been a stranger to off-roading or taking shortcuts on unmarked roads and dusty trails. But I wasn't accustomed to this type of off-roading. At times our SUV practically stood up vertically just to collapse over a bolder and then take a 45-degree deep dive into the void. Rinse and repeat for almost 5 hours! Luckily our driver Mo was competent and experienced at driving in this hostile terrain. There were a couple of close calls, but our bond grew stronger along the way.

# 4

# Kamawornie: Exploring the Outskirts and Learning About the Education System in Sierra Leone

Once we had arrived in Kamakwie, we were in desperate need for some downtime. The long and strenuous trip through the bush had left their imprint. Unavailable accommodations were just a subtle reminder that this was going to be the beginning of something bigger. It was late, and everything had turned pitch black. After some debating, Abu decided to walk across town to get in contact with the Wesleyan Secondary School authorities. After a short time, a small group of villagers and Abu appeared in the distance. Abu was able to secure us appropriate lodgings at one of the school principal's houses. Luckily, they were more than happy to open their home to a bunch of weary travelers.

Kamakwie wasn't well known for tourism of any kind. Tripadvisor gave a shout-out to the Northern Province that had highlighted Kamakwie as a charming town, but the available accommodations described there were inaccurate. The traveler-focused website made the local surroundings sound quaint but failed to mention the fact that life in these rural areas is all about fighting for survival. It soon became clear to me that the unsuspecting traveler would have been disappointed. Thankfully, I had come to understand my surroundings and appreciated the time I was able to spend in Sierra Leone. Embracing those daily challenges came easy to me, and I developed a deeper appreciation for the beautiful people of this bountiful country. Their seemingly indestructible positive outlook on life started rubbing off on me.

*Mother walking with her baby in Kamakwie*

Many of the rural Sierra Leonean inhabitants had never seen a white person in real life before. Their curiosity and genuine interest were something I hadn't experienced before. It was a very different kind of allure; interactions were heartfelt, warm, and welcoming. Naturally, some of the locals were suspicious and had their reservations. But being greeted by a flurry of hand-waving "hello's" as we were driving the country roads was a testimony to the people's genuine sincerity, warmth, and openheartedness. It also confirmed that I was correct in initiating my endeavor in this very deserving community.

*Red sand roads and busy traffic in Kamakwie*

Almost overnight it had gotten excessively humid, which was a sure sign that the monsoon season was about to start. The heat level had been rising mercilessly. To make things worse, the anticipated temperature drop that was forecasted didn't happen until 2:00 a.m. the following day. As the sun started coming up again at around 4:30 a.m., the heat set in soon thereafter.

My room didn't have any AC, and the fan was only working as long as there was electricity. We were far removed from the city, and electricity shut off every morning at 1:00 a.m. on the dot. Luckily, our host had installed tight-knit mesh over all windows to keep out pests and Malaria-carrying mosquitos. I tried to keep my window open for as long as possible at night. I found out quickly that the bathrooms didn't necessarily include a working shower or toilet paper but instead buckets of collected rainwater.

Life for a lot of Sierra Leoneans was demanding, but most people I had encountered on my trip were friendly, welcoming, and had smiles on their faces. We decided to go out for breakfast. Abu let us know that he had a childhood friend in town who owned a small restaurant. Apparently, their fish was renowned throughout the region. I was in dire need of a fresh cup of coffee and eagerly agreed to tag along.

Mo, our driver, Abu, and I walked to the restaurant for a late breakfast that day. Unfortunately, Mo didn't have time to join us for breakfast. Once we got to the place, he let us know that it was necessary to get the SUV geared up and ready for our upcoming travels. Apparently, the truck was in grave need of a whole new set of tires, "if we were going to continue with our trip at all," he said.

*Our SUV that withstood the rough off-road terrain, red-dirt roads,*
*and jungles of Sierra Leone*

"If you guys are intending to visit any of the other communities, meet with the representatives from the Wesleyan Secondary School, explore the National Park, and eventually head back to Freetown, then we will need four working mud tires," Mo was adamant. He looked wide-eyed as he gestured into the distance. Abu and I agreed that it was probably for the best to get prepared for a lot rockier terrain, especially since we also had planned on spending a couple of days commuting though the Outamba-Kilimi National Park.

*Finding new working tires at the local mechanic shop*

Entering the restaurant from the earthen road, unsuspecting patrons were promptly introduced to a small staircase that in turn opened into the dining room area. The dining area included five tables and was tastefully decorated. It was immediately apparent that the place was small but well-maintained. A wooden bar separated the dinette from the kitchen that extended into the back of the building.

The restaurant owner and her teenage daughter shared responsibilities. The mother prepared the food over an open fire in the back of the house, while the daughter looked after the customers with great attentiveness. Unsurprisingly, the menu contained a wide variety of dishes that included rice, yams, and eggs.

After Abu had introduced everybody, Adama, the restaurant owner, let us know that she was going to cook a special breakfast to give us strength for our upcoming tasks. At once, her daughter Fatmata left quickly to prepare fresh coffee for our table. Having had that flavorful strong coffee from the Freetown coffee shop, I had high hopes for another delightful cup of coffee.

As good as breakfast and upcoming dinners were in this fine establishment, I was dumbfounded to learn that the coffee was not at all what I had expected it to be. Nonetheless, it was what I had come to expect when frequenting diners in the United States. Every cup included a little coffee packet. Those instant single serves had a side of creamer, but sugar was already to be found on the table.

My mind started wandering. I recalled my first day in Freetown, when the coffee shop owner had counseled me about the ongoing shortage of agricultural exports, which included all coffee products. Naturally, my expectations coming to this West African country for the very first time were nearly non-existent. In retrospect, I was very fortunate to have had access to coffee most mornings during my stay in Sierra Leone.

It was only much later that I learned that most of the country's imported products were shipped into the Freetown Terminal, which served as the country's largest container port. It was also Africa's largest natural harbor, as well as main gateway for trade between Sierra Leone and the rest of the world. Unfortunately, now there were hardly any containers exporting Sierra Leonean coffee. Most of the coffee beans that were currently harvested had been planted before the war. Due to the number of farmers who had abandoned their farms during those war-torn years, there was very little coffee production or plant cultivation.

While I was checking my email on my phone, it occurred to me that almost everybody in this village seemed to have working Wi-Fi connections. Seeing a significant number of the younger generation exchanging information with their smartphones gave me hope for the future. Coffee production in 2022 had been down by 33% from the previous year, but it was clear to me that cellphone use was in full swing. Eventually, the anticipated computer lab needed to have 24/7 access to a working Wi-Fi connection. My excitement level instantly rose anticipating the upcoming meeting with the governing body of the local Wesleyan Secondary School.

Just as we were finishing up our breakfast, Mo reappeared to let us know that the SUV was ready to go. We decided that it would be best to take the rest of the day off to explore the neighboring towns and smaller communities such as Kamawornie.

The anticipated trip to Kamawornie turned out to be 100% off-road and featured some extreme inclines. It took us about 3 hours to get to that little village, but once we reached our destination it was well worth the extra effort. The village of Kamawornie was known to be the seat of the Chiefdom of Sella Limba. Our arrival was well-received, and the highest-ranking tribal leaders met with us in their traditional regalia. Their interest in our Western society, approachability, and hospitability was remarkable.

*Greeting the village chief of Kamawornie of the Sella Limba*
*Chiefdom dressed in tribal regalia*

Wearing regalia signifies respecting one's traditions and sacrifices made by their community. Oftentimes, leaders of a community wear tribal regalia for traditional ceremonial events and other formal or religious activities. I felt honored to be greeted and welcomed in this way. To me it signified the importance of our arrival and underscored how much the locals value and appreciate the help offered by the outside world.

After the initiation period, which included the traditional prayer and sharing of stories, some of Kamawornie's elders gave me a tour of their primary education buildings and the surrounding area. I learned that a lot of the children living in surrounding villages are offered an elementary school education in their school. Some of those 4- to 8-year-old kids must walk up to 5 miles every morning to reach the town of Kamawornie.

*Town of Kamawornie Elementary School visit*

Although some of the basic materials, such as books, chalk, and at times even chairs and desks, were scarce, the school made it a point to keep their doors open for all children willing to get a primary education. Their immediate goal was to add to the already existing structure and expand on their facilities to offer more kids the kind of education that would teach them how to read, write, and do basic arithmetic.

*Kamawornie Elementary School future expansion in progress*

With an anticipated expansion, the need for additional teachers would become pressing as well. Finding qualified staff and funds to pay salaries had been a challenge for quite some time. During times of hardship, when state funding was not available or was diminished, parents started contributing to teachers wages, even compensating them with cooked meals and groceries.

I also learned that faith played a big role in their school's curriculum. Kids were taught an appreciation for spirituality and indigenous religion early on. Over the course of my time in Sierra Leone, I gained an appreciation for its peoples and treasured traditions. Naturally, saying grace wasn't unexpected, but prayers that sanctified upcoming projects or friendships formed were surprising and appreciated.

# 5

# The Wesleyan Secondary School in Kamakwie

Our drive back to Kamakwie was rather uneventful. We decided not to visit any other towns that day and instead start focusing on what was ahead. The next morning, after making a routine stop at the now-cherished Adama's restaurant, we finally proceeded to the place we really came to see; namely, the Wesleyan Secondary School.

The school was situated on the outskirts of the Kamakwie. Lush greenery and an open-concept layout gave the school grounds a larger appearance than anticipated. I immediately felt that my awaited project could grow strong roots here.

The principal, Mr. Kandeh Bangura, greeted us. The plan had been to start off with a formal meet-and-greet. This was a favorable way for all parties that were going to be involved in this project to get to know one another.

*Our first preliminary meeting to discuss the Wesleyan
School addition objectives*

The Wesleyan School has a colorful history, as it had been established a long time before the Civil War. Although Kamakwie's main economic activities had been farming and trading, its inhabitants have been very keen on giving their youth a quality education.

This secondary school was a Christian, Wesleyan Methodist faith–based school. Their educational leaders believed in traditional morning greetings and prayers that conveyed the strong belief system at the school. Traditionally, the Wesleyan Methodist Connection was found in Utica, New York, in 1843. Their primary intent was based on the abolishment of slavery, and they were successful in promoting their belief system all throughout the United States, Canada, the UK, South Africa, Namibia, Sierra Leone, Liberia, Indonesia, and Australia.

The roots of their belief system are found in the teachings of John Wesley, and the Church headquarters are in Fishers, Indiana. I was also intrigued to learn that the Wesleyan Methodists not only advocated for abolition but also advocated for women's rights. They were extremely progressive for the time and found creative ways to promote their belief system. They sponsored traveling preachers led, most notably, by Rev. James Caughey to Ontario in the 1840s. His technique of "combined restrained emotionalism with a clear call for commitment" was adapted in the project of opening more sophisticated congregations in emerging cities.

During my lengthy meetings with Abu and the school superiors, I was pleased to find out that the town of Kamakwie was a host to other nonprofit organizations that assisted young women and mothers in getting a secondary education to improve their lives. It became apparent that the presence of the town's pastor, and the blessings given on several occasions throughout the day, were customary.

The Wesleyan Secondary School's grounds were rather large; nevertheless, finding an apparent space that was going to be suitable for our anticipated expansion was not an easy task. A lot of the buildings were still damaged from the Civil War, while others were not appropriate in terms of size or geographical location. My vision was to open the doors to a fully equipped computer laboratory that would serve all K-12 students as a brick-and-mortar facility as well as online classroom.

The GenHybrid Systems learning method originated from the necessity for a better learning model that could be applied to school systems in need. The underlying idea was to form a cohesive online/offline model that could serve students more efficiently and would increase their college entrance exam scores as well as acceptance rates.

*Our initial meeting at the Wesleyan Secondary School in Kamakwie
with their school leaders and pastor discussing the possibility of a computer
lab and classroom space*

Before and immediately after independence in 1827 the standard of education in Sierra Leone had been the highest of all of Africa; hence, it was dubbed the "Athens of West Africa." The continued erosion of its educational system between 1970 and 1985 as well as during the Civil War years that followed (1991–2002) forced their once-highly-esteemed educational system to collapse.

The updated 2020 National Curriculum Framework and Guidelines for Basic Education were dubbed the 6-3-3-4 structure and ended up dividing their education system into four stages of learning:

1. Six years of primary learning
2. Three years of junior education
3. Three years of senior secondary or technical vocational education
4. Four years of college or other tertiary education

This new and improved 6-3-3-4 system was supposed to make education more inclusive and accessible for young people. With improved learning outcomes, the goal has been to get more high school graduates into universities to receive a higher education. An improved job market and economic growth are long-term goals that can be achieved by making technology jobs available to the younger generation throughout Sierra Leone.

With a strong education history, sought-after natural resources, and a ready workforce, Sierra Leone should be a country on the verge of overcoming the "least developed" stigma that came with the United Nations label. Sierra Leone has been labeled a nation that is part of the so-called Fourth World, which essentially was attached to the most underdeveloped and poverty-stricken regions of the world. Although many "Fourth World" countries are rich in culture, traditions, and knowledge systems, their extremely low-income levels and minimum standard of living in rural areas attached a stigma to a lot of countries that otherwise would have been rated higher on the Gross Domestic Product (GDP), Gross National Product (GNP), and Mortality rate scales.

Those metrics don't tell the entire story. As a matter of fact, there has been loud criticism of the outdated First, Second, Third (and Fourth) categorizations. Increased Foreign Direct Investment (FDI) and freer trade agreements have been blurring the lines, and developing countries have been allowed to participate in the global economy more actively than they had been in the past.

Those overly simplified terms have led to misconceptions. China, Singapore, and Brazil have been categorized as "Second World" or developing, industrialized countries, but not "First World" countries due to the outdated rating system applied. India is still to this day labeled as "Third World," although their economy, with a GDP of $3.75 trillion, is the sixth largest worldwide.

I believe that today lines are getting blurred and outdated stigmas should be replaced. A country like Sierra Leone that has always been rich in natural resources and educational heritage should be on the verge of a "coming of age," as the transitional phase had already begun. In 2021, when my initial journey to Sierra Leone was underway, I fully anticipated traveling into a country that was poorly organized and in social disarray. To my surprise, I was greeted with openness that I had rarely experienced in the past traveling to other supposedly more developed nations that were, in the present political and economic climate, referred to as industrialized countries.

GenHybrid Systems was finally ready to gain some traction, and the social media team was ready to post daily updates and stimulate engagement. The overall positivity of the Sierra Leonean people and love for life were reflected in my pictures and videos. Posts came easily, and engagement seemed guaranteed.

# 6

# GenHybrid Systems Computer Lab

After numerous meetings and endless insightful discussions, we agreed on converting an existing building into a working computer lab with additional classroom space. The Wesleyan Secondary School leaders were overjoyed to find out that they were finally going to be able to offer computer training and classroom education to their students.

*A Wesleyan School representative giving us a tour*

The idea to be able to host in-classroom and online education for kids who might not be able to make it to school every day was tremendous. The principals let me know that this kind of hybrid education was going to be particularly helpful to the female student population of the school. I learned that girls are asked to help out with daily chores around the house and oftentimes get overlooked when families are planning to send their children for higher education. Frequently, due to hardship, parents can't support their kids any longer, and girls are left to their own devices at a very young age. Tragically, this often leaves girls with few employment options, and many end up turning to sex work or worse.

*Wesleyan Secondary School students walking outside of the anticipated
GenHybrid Systems computer lab building*

The norm for most of the female population had become a prospect-less future. Offering continued education, which would open new doors, could ignite hope and motivation. Develop Africa's CEO Sylvester, who was born and raised in Freetown, gave me additional insight into how the prospect of a better life and economic stability could change attitudes and would be a huge step in the right direction.

The country had been under duress for several years. Enabling K-12 students to create a better future for themselves and their families would benefit the entire nation. The main source of income for the country came from the exportation of minerals, agriculture, fisheries, and forestry. Although recognized as one of the top diamond producers in the world, Sierra Leone was faced with disproportionate exploitation throughout several economic sectors in the past. The same can be said for their forestry, or deforestation that are currently causing many natural disasters, including mudslides and landslides that lead to flooding all around the capital of Freetown.

Urbanization efforts led by foreign investors, as well as the devastating effects of mining on this country, have led to excessive deforestation. The physical consequences of this mindless activity have been health related. Due to the loss of forestry, interaction between humans and animals, also known as zoonoses, has led to outbreaks of several preventable diseases. Cholera, Measles, and a fruit-bat-originated Ebola virus are just the tip of the iceberg. Some of the more common diseases that have been linked to deforestation include Lassa virus, Lyme disease, Malaria, Zika virus, Marburg, and Henipavirus.

Unfortunately, the inhabitants of this beautiful country have been unable to find a way to free themselves from the claws of their investors, the lingering effects of the Civil War, as well as the greed of a small group of people who managed to profit from the many poor people of Sierra Leone. Farmers and other struggling, hardworking people have had to sell whatever they can just to survive. This vicious cycle could only be broken by offering better jobs, higher wages, and a real future for the younger generations of Sierra Leone.

This country was in dire need of change. Bringing GenHybrid Systems to the Wesleyan Secondary School in Kamakwie was going to be a start. We needed to create a space that was conducive to learning in-class and online. The idea sounded great in theory, but the execution of the idea was far more problematic.

To build a new school branch and to promote it to the authorities as something necessary, although it had never been in existence before, was an entirely different story. The administration of the Wesleyan Secondary School was overjoyed to help in the undertaking, but to make this official, we not only needed to write a new curriculum that included computer-based learning that had never been a part of the existing school system but also needed to gain approval from the governing Board of Education.

At this point I had to remind myself that Sierra Leone as a location for improved learning was the perfect place. Sylvester agreed with me that curriculum changes in Sierra Leone would not be as political as it might be in more developed parts of the world. The governing body might also be intrigued about the upcoming developments and computer-based education. We decided to take it one step at a time and start by planning how to convert the offered building into a computer-based facility. I was now aware of the huge number of smartphone users all over the country and their ability to use phones to the full extent of their capabilities.

One morning, sitting alone over breakfast in our favorite restaurant in Kamakwie, a couple of young men struck up a conversation with me. At this point I had gotten used to all the attention I got because a lot of rural Sierra Leoneans hadn't seen a white person before. That day at breakfast two young men speaking perfect English didn't seem to be too interested in my skin color. After a few short introductory remarks, they made it clear me that they had met white people in Sierra Leone before, but those other white people were more interested in their country's natural resources. They explained to me that it was rare to find white people so far out in rural Sierra Leone.

The taller and more outspoken of the two young men introduced himself as Ibrahim. He seemed very fascinated with the idea of starting an addition in the form of a computer lab and classroom at the Wesleyan Secondary School.

"That is a great idea," he said without hesitation.

Finally, after hearing my story and mulling it over for a while, his reserved friend decided to join in on our conversation.

"I agree with Ibrahim. My name is Adan"; after briefly shaking hands, he continued, "that is something this school has tried to implement for many years but to no avail. When I was a sophomore in high school, they wanted to make computers available to all students, but as far as I can remember, nothing ever materialized. I wish you would have come here five years ago." Both men started laughing, their beautiful teeth flashing.

Admittedly, I was impressed with their natural way of conducting themselves and, despite their youth, their maturity. After a brief period of silence, I decided to get their opinion about hybrid learning in Sierra Leone.

"So, Adan and Ibrahim, what do you know about hybrid learning?"

"Oh," Ibrahim interjected as soon as I had spoken the last syllable, "I know that with the pandemic hybrid learning has become a very popular choice for many schools out there."

"That is what I have heard as well," Adan added.

"Okay, but do you guys think that this is something you could see K-12 kids gravitating toward here in Kamakwie or anywhere in Sierra Leone for that matter?"

After another moment of silence and exchanged glances, the boys started talking at the same time: "Well, yes, why wouldn't they?" Both were looking intently at me. "This is something we need to have available at all schools here in Sierra Leone. Just like Adan already said, I wish we would have had that technology available when we went to high school back then," Ibrahim was looking at Adan for additional input.

"I believe here in Kamakwie, we live a little off the beaten path," Adan took the invitation to start adding the conversation. "The Freetown administration that is responsible for education all around the country is, in all honesty, only interested in providing for their city's people. They don't really care too much about the rural areas. This is why I think you really are making a difference. Nobody within the board of education really wants to deal with us. The bigger problem is that most of the funding goes to Freetown schools."

I was a little shocked to hear so much candidness from the two young men and didn't mind that my breakfast was getting cold. After taking a few sips of coffee and gathering my thoughts, I said, "Well, from where I'm standing your life here in the countryside seems to be healthier overall compared to Freetown. The slower pace of life here should allow more time for education. It might just be a matter of getting more organized and getting qualified teachers to come here."

Ibrahim and Adan again started bursting out laughing. It was refreshing to hear.

"Well," Ibrahim was trying to get his composure back, "why did you come all the way out here then?"

After gathering my thoughts for a few seconds, I let them know that it was the best possible solution for everybody involved. It didn't come across as an honest enough answer, so I tried again.

"Okay, so my organization needed to partner with a local group to turn this dream of mine into reality. Freetown schools were not as forthcoming and had demands that I wasn't willing to meet. Develop Africa had already established connections with the Wesleyan Secondary School. So, this was not only an easy transition, but also something that made a lot of sense looking back."

"Ha," Ibrahim exclaimed, "so you are really only doing this here purely by accident then."

I started to feel a little bit uncomfortable as both their expressions changed, only to follow up with another loud laugh.

"Ibrahim is only messing with you," Adan said, putting his hand on my shoulder. "We think that this is really great, what you are trying to do here."

"Of course, man," Ibrahim added. "This is a hell of a thing. Nobody else ever came here. To add to your theory that we are living healthier and all that, yes to an extent. But who cares about fresh air when you don't have money to eat? We don't have the wildlife we used to have, and farming is also not a thing for most people anymore ever since the Civil War. Did you know that they held the Wesleyans hostage back then? Anyways, the biggest thing really is getting a perspective, man. What about us having a real future? You can only get a future with a solid understanding of technology nowadays."

"Ain't that the truth," Adan cried. "Without that you aren't qualified to do anything anymore. Look, Chris, we don't have the farming anymore, and tourism is also not a thing here. In case you wondered, we are just visiting our families here because we are studying business in Lagos. Things are really picking up over there. Once you graduate, the best thing for you, and your family, is to leave."

Again, their words were raining down on me, and I started to feel their effects. The honesty and the pain laid out so plainly in front of me—it was a lot to take in. I wished that I could do more for them, for the entire country really. It was just so unjust, and for a moment I felt like I had failed them. I knew that I couldn't take on all their problems, but I really longed to make a difference, more than just adding that computer lab or adding classroom space. I now understood that the problem was just so much bigger, and all these people ever knew was exploitation, even by their own people.

After another minute or so I had caught hold of myself again and said, "Yes, you guys are right. It does seem a little hopeless, doesn't it?"

Both of my friends suddenly put their arms around me, and Ibrahim yelled out, "If all white people that come to this country would be more like you, we would be the richest country in the world."

At this point I started crying. What was going on with me? This hadn't happened in many, many years. I was almost beside myself. The realness of it all was just so new to me. I couldn't hold it in any longer and had to wipe my face to keep the tears from dripping onto my cold breakfast.

"Wow, guys. What is happening with me?"

"Don't you worry about that. Only real men cry!" Both of my friends started laughing out loud again. It was so contagious that I had to join them. What a crazy day it had shaped up to be.

"Hey, Chris, let me just add this before we leave you to your breakfast," Adan said while another quick smile flew over his face. "You remember how we let you know earlier on in our conversation that other white men have come this far out, but they were interested in our natural resources, diamonds in particular?"

"Yes," I said.

"Well, those people are not the kind of people we like to attract, but that is still our bread and butter here. Without our minerals this country would have completely fallen off the map by now. It would be great if we could one day be like a lot of the other more developed African nations and offer our younger generations computer classes at all schools throughout the country. Maybe that is something you could let your fellow Americans know when you go back to your country."

I looked at my two new friends in amazement. "Well, I intend to do that, and it's really great to have met you two." I almost felt sad that they had to leave.

"Don't worry, Chris, I know that this is just the beginning of something. Have you seen that movie, *Blood Diamond*?"

Both of my friends gave me a final hug before leaving. I felt richer and more accomplished for some strange reason than I had ever felt before. How strange was that?

*Ibrahim (left) and Adan (right)*

# 7

# Making It Happen

With my newfound energy, I decided to start fresh with an invigorated and positive outlook. Meeting Ibrahim and Adan was not just a chance encounter. I had to believe that it was fate. It was almost as if the universe was letting me know to hurry up already and get this thing started. Now, I had the motivation I needed to see this through, and for the first time I truly felt that classes had to start that upcoming school year—no matter what.

I took out my old little black leather-bound notebook and started making a list of things we needed to get for the dedicated school building to turn it into the GenHybrid Systems computer lab building. Here is what I came up with:

**Cleanup of the Surrounding Area and Interior:** One of the rooms inside the building was hosting an old rotary printing press. At one point it may have been used for offset printing. The plan was to turn the main room or parlor into a working computer lab. Judging from the current condition it was in, the space hadn't been used in quite some time and was in desperate need of some TLC.

**Renovations of the GenHybrid Systems Building:** The roof had been leaking and needed to be partially replaced. The windows were outdated, and some were not operational. After speaking to the Wesleyan School representatives and Pastor Daniel, who was really helpful, I was assured that it would be beneficial to think about added security for the GenHybrid Systems building. Although the town of Kamakwie was peaceful and people were respectful of school property, bars on the windows would surely send the right signal as well as protect the space from strong winds and other unforeseen natural disasters.

The interior and exterior of the building needed a fresh coat of paint as well. Most buildings on Wesleyan Secondary School's grounds were either tan or a muted shade of brown. We decided to give the computer lab exterior a more updated look and went with a black-and-white theme throughout. Once completed, the stark contrast really made the building stand apart from the rest of the buildings, serving as a focal point, which was part of the strategy to begin with.

*Updated black-and-white exterior paint for the GenHybrid computer lab*

The front entrance to the building was in dire need of restoration. We decided to do some concrete resurfacing to give the porch a new finish. The rainy season in Sierra Leone, which traditionally lasts from June till September, can be devastating. It made a lot of sense to add an additional 3-inch layer of concrete to fill in all the cracks and make the porch more respectable looking. A long-term goal was to eventually make the building's surrounding area a social meeting ground for computer, IT, and media and tech students.

**Computer Lab Setup:** The building didn't have working power. My first thought was to get a solar-powered system in place. After connecting with some of the local solar providers, it became clear that this might be future project. To get this project operational, we decided to go the conventional route and started running electrical wire though the building and utilizing HP 135 Watt power supplies.

*Local construction crew resurfacing the GenHybrid
computer lab building patio*

After the electrical installation was completed, the interior of the building needed to be attended to. The flooring was in bad shape, the walls were rough, and the ceiling also showed wear and tear in the form of cracks that had been getting bigger over the course of time.

Once the AC connectors were put in place, we were able to start thinking about classroom management. Purchasing Microsoft servers that could be used to store and share information between the students and instructors was necessary. The Develop Africa representatives let me know that all their office spaces, which included regular courses taught to improve skills, had servers installed. Server management and updating was something common and useful as an educational tool for young students.

My personal expectations were to educate K-12 students on the basic uses of computer systems: how to store and retrieve data and how to operate computer applications. We decided that once students got familiar with computer operations, an entry-level class on typing documents, sending emails, and using the web effectively as a research tool would be a great starting point. How to turn on a computer was the basic starting point. Familiarity with using computer graphics applications as a way to create computer-generated art for advanced classes was the goal.

Of course, we were going to have to hire competent instructors at some point, and the curriculum was going to include computer classes as well. It was easy to get carried away in the process. We had to remind ourselves that the computer lab was far from done.

*Sending computer equipment via bulk mail to Sierra Leone*

Once the structure itself was starting to resemble an actual laboratory, we needed to think about what kind of computer equipment we were going to purchase for the school. Of course, we also had to keep in mind that some of the classes were going to be taught as hybrid classes. We decided to go with PCs over Macintosh computers. After a lengthy discussion it became clear that Sierra Leone was better equipped to keep a PC-based computer lab updated and running smoothly over time.

I remembered some of the discussions I had early on with Sylvester about Hewlett Packard (HP) computers and his positive experiences with using them for his employees' continuing education seminars. Maybe I was going to be able to find bulk offerings on eBay for 25 to 30 upgradable HP computers. After doing a little research on my phone I noticed that most bulk offers didn't come with any kind of hardware, keyboards, or mice. This project was getting more and more involved.

Adding much-needed headsets to every computer station was going to be a good starting point to integrate the hybrid experience. Students who were not going to be able to walk to school every day could log in from phones or tablets in their homes. Hybrid classes required headsets, so that everybody could communicate with each other. I was very excited to see hybrid learning developing in Sierra Leone.

*Computers were gathered and checked in Freetown before being sent to the Wesleyan School in Kamakwie*

Of course, the idea of integrating online learning had been on my mind a long time before the pandemic caused educators to rethink learning methodologies. Having been raised in Germany in a rigid educational system during the pre-internet days, for me the online tools that had become available to us in the early 2000s provided possibilities to improve education for young minds all over the globe.

One of the first and most obvious changes that came to mind was the learning that kids from various cultures could provide for each other. For example, I envisioned an elementary school kid from Indonesia talking about their culture, habits, and interests to another child from Sierra Leone, who in turn would share their beliefs and customs. This real-time learning and sharing of information could have an enormous impact on how kids perceive their current environment and possible future. Naturally, children from developing countries could benefit the most from technology. Otherwise, limited resources keep a large percentage of children from graduating from high school or even middle school.

Data suggested that girls would have a more difficult time in life than boys if they didn't graduate. The negative impact of dropping out of school before graduation would make girls' futures bleak. The idea of offering tablet checkouts for a limited amount of time was something we could integrate as well. Despite my positive outlook, I needed to remind myself that there was a limited amount of funding available, and we couldn't afford to lose equipment during our first year.

This is how my list slowly came alive. My thoughts started drifting to all the places I still wanted to visit, but I needed to maintain focus. There were still a lot of adventures to be had, but, without a complete list and a clear plan to move ahead, this undertaking would never see the light of day. Outside of all the technology that was going to be invested into the computer lab, we also needed to start thinking about Wi-Fi providers that were going to serve our rural Kamakwie community, which was far outside of the city limits.

After talking with some of the schools' representatives and Mo, our driver (who turned out to be very knowledgeable about technological advancements made in West Africa), Orange SL materialized as the best and most reliable network connectivity in Sierra Leone. Mo also advised me on matters concerning computer specifications and possible classes that could be offered as a good starting point. Mo, who let me know that he built computers "for extra cash" in his spare time and who was also savvy in fixing "anything related to phones," told me that the key to our success would be how the school was received by the student body within the first six months or so.

Those were the thoughts I was contemplating while trying to get my list completed. As for the computers themselves, they needed to have sufficient RAM to run all the applications that we were planning on using for beginners as well as for more advanced graphics students. We also needed fast processors

(CPU) and good working graphic cards (GPU) to ensure that the highest form of computer-based education could be offered. I already knew that the younger Sierra Leonean generation was eager to become computer savvy.

Up to this point of my stay in this beautiful West African country, I had already had many discussions with young adults who were more than happy to share their knowledge and insight into the inner workings of their country's educational system. It became clear to me that the computer lab had to be sustainable and easy to update locally. After my visits to rural Sierra Leone and meetings with school representatives, it was clear that even chairs and tables were difficult to come by.

The chosen building had three large rooms and one smaller storage facility. Two of the rooms were filled with a lot of stuff I hadn't examined yet. Partly because we were partial to the idea of turning the bigger third room into the computer lab. Now, after having had some time to sit and reflect, it occurred to me that the first room, although filled with junk, already had concrete desks in place. When that room was used for printing, somebody must have thought it wise to install the desks. This would be a far better choice for classroom purposes. The larger first room could be turned into the anticipated library instead, and the adjacent room would be additional classroom space.

As I was jotting down those last ideas, I suddenly felt an overwhelming sense of purpose and desire to see this project come to life. Things did fall into place when the right amount of work and time were invested. I felt like I was shaping my own destiny. It was a great feeling, and I decided right then and there that if I had had any doubt before, now I knew that I was going to see this through to the end.

This was the path I decided to forge for myself and the Wesleyan Secondary School. It was time to get the manpower, materials, and equipment needed to turn this dream into reality. I planned on seeing the school and walking the school grounds one more time before catching my flight back the following week. During the remaining few days, I wanted to do a little more sightseeing. The first thing on my list was visiting the Outamba-Kilimi National Park.

# 8

# Outamba-Kilimi National Park

We got together as a group the following morning to make plans to drive to the Outamba-Kilimi National Park. I had been looking forward to this trip for a long time. It was a welcome change of pace from the school project we had been working on for weeks. This venture would be something I had dreamed of doing ever since I was a little kid. Seeing hippos, monkeys, elephants, or the African blue flycatcher roaming around in the wild would make the trip a complete success.

Mo started packing the necessary gear in case of an emergency. He said that the toughest part of the trip might be just getting there: "Do you remember the road leading to Kamakwie out of Freetown?" Oh, did I remember that seemingly never-ending, off-roading experience? Yes, naturally I did and probably will for the rest of my life.

"Oh, the trip leading to the Natural Reserve will be far worse than what you experienced coming up North," Mo said.

With those words he turned away and started loading gallons of fuel into the SUV. He was very focused and didn't seem too distracted by all the activity going on around him. We had decided to stay a couple of days in that neighborhood. The park bordered on the Republic of Guinea, and, as Mo had already pointed out, it was not easy to access.

At this point the rainy season still hadn't begun, and we were trying to avoid bad weather at all costs. It appeared that there wasn't going to be any rain in the forecast, but, as Abu let me know, the weather was unpredictable this time of the year and could change at any moment. West Africa, especially Sierra Leone, had massive soil erosion because of deforestation. Abu further explained that China had a big influence on their country's economy and general well-being.

The Chinese government started taking advantage of Sierra Leone's need for foreign help. The cost of Chinese "intervention" has been very high. When I was shopping around for solar panel options, I started noticing the hesitant but constant reminders that "it would be better to go with a local and not foreign company." At first, I thought that it made perfect sense that locals would suggest their own establishments over some foreign entity. After multiple reminders over the course of two weeks of shopping, I realized that although local firms wouldn't be able to compete with the Chinese prices and guarantees given, it wouldn't be advisable for me to go that route.

Local people realized that their government was selling them out and were willing to fight back, despite the betrayal by their politicians. At one point I had made an appointment to meet with a managing Chinese representative to negotiate a deal for solar power. After a lengthy meeting, I was told that my offer also had to be approved by the Chinese party located in their home country and approval might take a while. A wise man once said that certain things in life couldn't be learned but had to be experienced. This may have been one of those instances.

At the very least I now could say that I had started to understand local ways. Chinese intervention had the potential to cripple the entire African continent, and the Chinese were more than happy to claim even the scraps as their own. Abu let me know that a lot of the major cities throughout Africa had already become more like Chinese cityscapes, complete with Chinese sculptures erected as symbols of economic superiority and dominance. It was apparent that the African continent was a battlefield of corporate takeover, and the Chinese seemed to be winning. I was appalled by the idea that Sierra Leonean officials seemed to be abandoning their duties to pocket additional funds for their own well-being.

Our drive to the Outamba-Kilimi National Park was the expected "rough ride." As we climbed 3- to 4-foot rocks, I started noticing the advanced deforestation extended into the rainforest and beyond. Abu and Mo didn't hesitate to point out the potentially devastating effects continued deforestation might have on the overall ecosystem. I had to admit that I was expecting some form of clear-cutting based on my most recent experiences, but nothing could have prepared me for the sheer magnitude of the loss of entire forests, which were home to unique wildlife for countless generations. Seeing the exposed and bare land was a truly heart-wrenching experience.

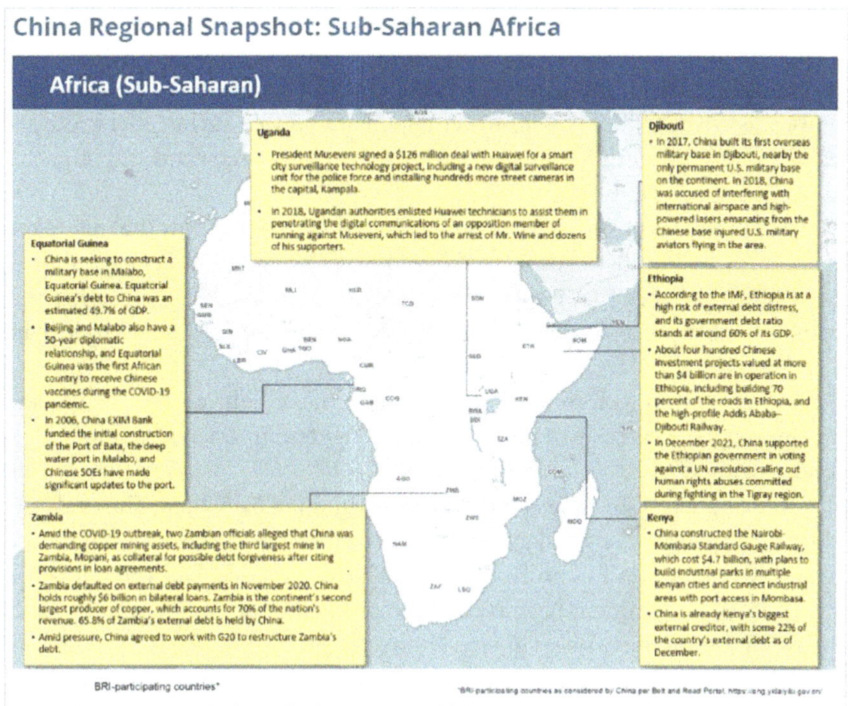


*China's strategic investments into African nations to further their own ends*

We took several breaks on the trip to stretch our aching backs and to give our trusty SUV a break. Inching closer to the park, I decided to venture out on my own to get a better look at my surroundings. It was very apparent that mining was another cause of the ongoing deforestation. Looking over the exposed land, bulldozers were everywhere. Mo, who had come over to join me, lifted his hand and pointed north across the open land, saying, "That point over there where the hillside slightly dips is considered the entrance to the park."

I took another long look at all the burned trees and chopped-up logs paving the way to the entrance of the park.

"Mo, does this continue into the park? I thought that the park was protected," I asked.

"Well, yes, you are correct, but nobody can keep them from unlawfully running their quarries. The Chinese have added to the infrastructure and job market quite a bit over the last few decades. The problem is that the environment has paid the price for our wrongdoings."

"When you say, 'our wrongdoings,' you mean Chinese exploitation, don't you?"

"Well, that and the encouragement of our policymakers. Our country has a lot of natural resources, in particular granite. Most of the deforestation is due to Chinese granite mining, but this is very much encouraged by the people in power here. The Outamba-Kilimi National Park, as well as the other protected parks like the Western Peninsula Park that you haven't seen, are also impacted by corruption."

As I stood there speechless, Mo continued, "Did you know that our Western Peninsula Park was considered by UNESCO as a world heritage site? At one point I believed that more strict regulations enforced by the government could possibly prevent what you see here from happening. I now know that I was wrong."

"Why? I think you were on to something there. Your current regulations are inviting exploiters to take advantage. Tightening up restrictions might force a change."

Mo laughed, "This is exactly what I was thinking back then. The challenge is that our government will grant permits to the Chinese for the right price, regardless of any kind of protected status given to a place. Did you know that the Chinese government has invested around $6 billion in our country since 2010? You would have never guessed it, would you?"

"That can't be right, Mo. Do you know how much money that is?"

"Yes, I'm not stupid. Of course, I know how much money that is. It is $6 billion with a capital 'B'. It is enough money to tear down this entire country and rebuild it Google style."

Now it was my turn to laugh, "Did you say Google style? So, you think that $6 billion would get you a high-tech infrastructure for the entire country. You know, in all honesty, though, I really can't see where any of that money has gone. The only real city in Sierra Leone seems to be Freetown. I don't see that much money in improvements in or around Freetown. If you ask me, the architecture, electrical grid, roads, and landscape look very dated and in need of updating. And your airport—a throwback to the 1960s."

"Chris, please don't hold back," Mo said with a wide grin on his face.

"Well, I certainly mean no disrespect, but just look at the condition of the streets coming up to Kamakwie or coming out here to the Park. It's ridiculous. There is no money for public education, and entire neighborhoods in Freetown are abandoned. Obviously, if there was such astronomical funding, it went into the wrong pockets."

"Now you are catching on my friend; therein lies the problem. We all are aware of Chinese motives. They are already evident in Djibouti, Angola, Republic of Congo, Cameroon, Ethiopia, Kenya, and Zambia, just to mention a few countries that are almost completely owned by the Chinese now. When

China started coming into the picture as an investor during the 1980s, a large part of Sub-Saharan Africa was at risk. The Paris Club was not ready to intervene to the extent that was required. In the end, a lot of foreign investors started chipping in, and China made up the difference. At that point the intervention was appreciated. Have you ever heard of the Paris Club?"

"Well, yes, an informal group of countries that wanted to stabilize countries that were in need. They offered to find ways of handling the accumulated debt. I believe they were founded in the 1950s."

"Unfortunately, over the past 20 years or so there hasn't been a 'way of handling the accumulated debt', which is why China was able to take the lead in our country and the rest of Sub-Saharan Africa."

"Ah, so what other options were there available if not to take Chinese loans that couldn't have been repaid anyhow?" I wondered, realizing that China had handed out more money to African nations over the course of the last few decades than even the World Bank was able to.

"It does feel like we are stuck in a hopeless situation at times. But you know, Chris, our nation has been able to persevere and come back even stronger from a lot challenging situations. This is why you see people smiling. We don't dwell on things that can't be changed or are out of our control. My people are God-fearing, and we believe that eventually good things will come to us. In the meantime, we stay positive and fight the good fight."

While listening to Mo, I started to believe that he knew something that the rest of the world wasn't aware of. Abu had joined our meeting, but decided to be an observer, finally letting us know that it was getting late in the day and that it was time to push on. I agreed because I was getting anxious to see the wildlife of Sierra Leone.

Hitting the road again, my travel companions and I had to endure another stretch of extreme inclines and sketchy descents over rocky terrain before finally reaching the entrance of the Park. I couldn't believe that we had finally made it to our destination. Walking toward the entrance, I noticed a sign that read, "Mining, hunting, farming activities are not allowed." Then there was a second warning sign that let us know that there might be an Ebola outbreak in the area.

As Abu stepped out of the SUV, pointing with an outstretched hand toward the signs, he said that this was exactly the reason deforestation should be absolutely forbidden: "Not only does deforestation hurt our ecosystem and cause erosion and mudslides, but it also creates a festering ground for diseases. As you know, we have a mosquito problem in West Africa. The loss of our forests serves as an incubator for mosquito-borne sicknesses, and causes Ebola, Malaria, and Dengue fever to spread at lightning speed."

*Diseases like Ebola have been running rampant in Sierra Leone and all throughout West Africa largely due to deforestation*

Walking into the park, we decided to start enjoying our trip and to put our grumblings aside for the time being. We were greeted by a few park rangers who handed out life vests for the river raft and gave us detailed instructions on how to conduct ourselves inside the park. Mo and Abu warned me to stay calm and not to leave the boat in case of hippo sightings.

"This is something a lot of people in distress forget—even locals," emphasized Abu with a raised voice, "hippos look very cute and friendly but are really the most ferocious creatures in the entire jungle."

"Yes, Abu is right," Mo confirmed, "There are plenty of accidents that happen here every year, mostly because people don't respect hippo territory or just ignore the fact that hippos are known to attack humans all the time."

Mo and Abu were ready to add another warning but decided to dedicate their full attention to their life vests. I had a little extra time while everybody was still busy preparing for our upcoming river-rafting trip. I decided to ask one of our tour guides for more information on engaging with hippos in their natural habitat. Naturally, I started wondering if all the fuss about our little boating-and-hiking tour was exaggerated.

*Inside the National Park on our raft heading toward the hippo pool*

The first tour guide I approached was more than happy to confirm the information I had already been given by Mo and Abu. He said that there were several hundred people who died every year from hippo attacks throughout Africa. At the same time, Sierra Leone hadn't seen any in long time because there hadn't been many of hippos around since the early 2000s. They were considered an endangered species, and conservation efforts had been put into place with limited impact.

"Pigmy hippos have been threatened over the last couple of decades, primarily by loss of their territory. Our forests are disappearing, and poaching and hunting for bush meat is impacting their numbers as well," the guide shared.

It was apparent that the tour guide was starting to look dejected, while trying to share all the important facts with me.

"Yes, although the Upper Guinea Tropical Rainforest in south-eastern Sierra Leone was part of the first national community conservation program that was managed by Tiwai Island Administrative Committee, poaching and development was still going strong. Just to put that into perspective, the TIAC doesn't only represent our communities, but also the government, universities, and conservation organizations."

Once again, I was overcome with this sense of despair. It became increasingly difficult to maintain a positive outlook with all this destruction going on around me. But the tour guide gave me one of those big Sierra Leonean smiles that I had gotten so accustomed to, and added, "You know, we just must keep on reminding ourselves that we are truly blessed just to be here. Other places all around the world have it far worse than we do. We have this beautiful land, fresh air, and our country is filled with caring people. What more can we ask for?"

*Abu getting his life vest and water supply ready for the trip down the river*

Once we got ready and finally pushed off, paddling down the river, the scene was tranquil. It was hard to imagine that anything out of the ordinary or even monstrous could possibly happen to us out here. The water was calm, and the constant bird chatter followed us on our trip down the Kabba River. We decided to just enjoy the scenery and refrain from talking for the next couple of hours.

*Our view down the Kabba River on our search for wildlife*

It was a mesmerizing experience, and I was already looking forward to our canoe ride back. Once we arrived at a little bay that also featured a campground, the tour guides decided to make a stop. We got off the boat and started wading through the water until our feet hit solid ground. I caught sight of a narrow path that led back into the bush. The tour guides let us know that we should stay on the path to make our way safely through the Park.

"We have a lot of wildlife that can be seen close-up, but we must be careful. This park is a true sanctuary for wildlife, but it can come at a high cost. You can see birds, chimpanzees, and colobus monkeys hanging off trees, but we are also the host of ten of the most poisonous snakes in all of Africa. Gaboon Viper and the Western Green Mamba bites are deadly," the guide warned. "During the rainy season we lose a lot of farmers to snakebites. Once again, please be cautious, keep your eyes open, and stay on the dedicated path."

At this point, we had already entered the bush, and everybody seemed to be feeling fairly comfortable within the environment. The first thing that we started taking note of was the number of mango trees. Their abundance wasn't something I hadn't seen before. Spring sees a lot of Keit, Common, and Laberu mangoes ripening, but our tour guides were eager to add that peak mango season really only started in July.

I learned that mango production in Sierra Leone is not only a delicious and fun undertaking, but it can also be a great provider for the entire family. Mo added that in his younger years, they used sticks and stones to knock them out of trees. They would just start falling off, almost without any resistance. Occasionally, he had to climb those trees and start shaking branches to make the juicy and perfectly ripened fruit fall to the ground.

"You know, here in Salone the oldest siblings are in charge of climbing trees to get things moving," Mo loudly pronounced.

Judging from the roaring reaction the comment received from the group, Mo must have been spot-on in his observation. Sahr, one of our tour guides, pulled me aside. He explained that the very popular local moonshine palm wine, better known as "poyo" among the locals, was produced in all parts of Sierra Leone and it was seen an important aspect of their native culture. The oldest male siblings also had to climb palm trees to reach the very top and tap into the white, sweet sap.

"We have some poyo back at our station. Once we return, I will be happy to share a cup with all of you," Sahr said. He received a lot of goodwill and cheers from our group for his very generous offer. He further explained that the Limba people, one of the oldest ethnic groups in Sierra Leone, believed that "he who brings poyo, brings joy to the family." It was very apparent that people in Salone relish social gatherings and spending time with loved ones. They also don't mind sharing a few cups of poyo while telling stories and having a good time.

*Abu, Sahr, and me enjoying some poyo*

*Cheers!*

As we started walking deeper into the Park, we could hear a wide diversity of birds and their sounds. Sahr let us know that the West African region of Sierra Leone was home to approximately 680 different species of birds. As we approached our first resting spot, I turned to the tour guides and asked: "How likely is it that we will be able to spot a Martial Eagle around here?"

"Oh, my friend," Sahr joyfully said, "if we were to spot one of those great hunters, it would be our lucky day indeed."

As we started taking seats on tree stumps, fallen branches, or on one of the many protruding roots, Sahr continued to elaborate on the presence and significance of the Martial Eagle in Sierra Leone and on the entire African continent: "You know, they are known to be found in forest areas such as this park because they tend to breed in bush regions high up on the tallest trees."

Sahr was taken by my interest in the Martial Eagle and decided to give me a little more inside information: "Growing up here in on the northern part of Sierra Leone, my dad and I used to travel around quite a bit because of his business. I was always happy to help and learn as much as I could. We would sometimes see this powerful raptor fly over our heads as we were driving along the countryside. One time I saw one just drop out of the sky only about twenty feet from us and pick up a jackal like it was nothing. What an amazing creature! He was completely white with dark wings and looked gigantic. If I had to guess, his wingspan was at least six feet. Why are you so interested in these birds, by the way?"

I wasn't really sure how to answer that question and decided to be as honest as I could: "Well, growing up in Germany I saw an eagle out in the open one time. I was still a young boy living with my family in Frankfurt. Germany used to have a lot of snow in the winter, and in December we often went sledding down the Great Field Mountain. As we were climbing up that mountain one Sunday morning, I saw that White-Tailed Eagle slowly hovering over us as it was gliding through the air. I just never forgot that experience. The Martial Eagle is of course far bigger and more menacing than any European eagle."

"Oh, I see. My dad told me that he saw the Martial Eagle pick up a small alligator when he was growing up in Kenya. Did you know that here in Sierra Leone we believe that the Martial Eagle can guide us to find deeper meaning in life or in situations of uncertainty?"

"No, I wasn't aware of that," I admitted. I was a little surprised by his spiritual interjection.

"Here in Africa, we believe that eagles have healing power, and the fact that you came here with the intention of seeing our great Martial Eagle makes me believe that he is going to guide you on your search for whatever you came to do here in Sierra Leone," he said.

Well, there was a lot that I still needed to do, but for now I felt content just navigating the Park and taking in all the natural beauty. Although most native people of Salone were known to be deeply religious, they also respected personal freedom and, therefore, practiced religious tolerance. It was customary to show deference for one another, regardless of religious belief. Sierra Leone's people believe that personal choice should be valued, which is evident in the high number of interreligious marriages.

Sahr gave me one of his big smiles and gleefully said, "Luckily, we brought plenty of water. Keep on hydrating. We still have a long hike ahead of us. In case you want to try some of the local fruit, feel free to pull down one of these branches and enjoy a sweet mango. Those are plentiful here, and we love them."

"Oh, yes, I already told him about our love for mangoes—haven't I, Chris?" Mo was eager to join our conversation.

"Yes, you told me about all the mangoes. I would think that the number of mango trees in Sierra Leone would mean that exporting them would make for a nice profit." (After sampling one of the mangoes, I have to add here that this was easily the best mango I had ever eaten in my life.)

"You would think that we had already figured that out, wouldn't you?" Abu hastily interjected. "Well, as it turns out, we are not really known as a mango-exporting country. We love to consume our own mangoes, but surprisingly enough we don't export them much at all. But you are correct; we should be one of the main exporters of mangoes in all of West Africa. I have said that for the longest time."

As Abu continued to state his case, we carried on with our hike. The temperature was rising as the day progressed, and we decided to take more frequent water breaks.

"You know, Chris, my family always had fresh, boiled, or dried mangoes around the house. Now, for example, freshly squeezed mango juice would be perfect."

Mo shot Abu a quick glance, "Stop talking about mango juice. Yes, an ice-cold mango juice would be really nice right now. Unfortunately, we are not close enough to being finished with our hike to be thinking about that right now, are we?"

Abu started laughing and then continued, "Well, yes, of course. Let me just say one more thing: Just as we are harvesting mangos locally, we could be selling them internationally. We only have one real mango exporter. They are in Freetown—Africa Felix Juice Factory. AFJ collects their supply from local farmers and then sells the juice concentrate to Europe and the US. They are a monopoly, and we still don't have anybody who exports fresh mangoes. Everything here takes forever, and people just don't have the resources to go and try things on their own."

*Picking fresh mangos from trees during our hike through the Outamba-Kilimi National Park (from left to right: Sahr, me, and Mo)*

For the next few miles, we continued our walk in silence, maybe because everybody was thinking about the possibility of marketing mangoes or maybe because nobody wanted to talk about ice-cold mango juice for fear of getting yelled at by Mo. The humidity was stifling, and the thought of drinking a cold mango juice was excruciating.

I wasn't acclimated yet, and my legs felt heavy as I tried to keep up with everyone else's pace. They were pushing forward to make it back in time to the boat by nightfall. The plan had been to stay at a nearby resort or campground for another day or so. After walking land inwards for a few hours and taking pictures of the wildlife, we decided to turn around and find our way back to our SUV once again.

This time of the year the sun was starting to set at around 7:00 p.m. Once the sun set, it quickly turned pitch black. The sky filled with countless stars that seemed to be hanging right over our heads. We were still walking as strange sounds started filling the air. We stayed the course, and as we arrived at the waterfront, the boatmen greeted us.

"How was your hike?" one of the boat operators asked me.

"Oh, it was quite an adventure, but I am ready to take a nap." Everybody seemed exhausted. We agreed to drive back that night. I was grateful to get back and get some rest, but at the same time I knew that I would come to miss this part of the world soon.

As we pushed off again, everybody agreed that we should have left for the park earlier in the day to avoid strenuous hiking during the worst part of the daytime heat. The terrain had been largely foothills with steep inclines and rocky mountainous terrain. I also took note that better gear and more water would be needed on our next excursion.

We got back to our truck very late that night, and nobody was really in a talking mood. As we took off, I remembered how long and tiresome the ride had been to the Park. I knew that I wouldn't be able to sleep in the truck because of the rough terrain. Besides, what would my newfound friends think of me? No, I just had to suck it up and try to stay awake.

Just as I was thinking what an outstanding job Mo was doing of taking us through the ups and downs of the outlandishly rough path leading back to Kamakwie, we saw two motorcyclists stranded by the side of the road. It was so dark that we almost ran into them. At the very last second Mo hit the breaks to avoid a crash. The truck came to a complete stop, and everybody exited to meet the two bikers who were already standing in front of the glaring headlights to greet us.

"What's good?" Mo was the first to approach the fellow travelers. It seemed as though we were all too worn out to think of any possible danger from this encounter in the middle of the jungle at this godforsaken hour of the night.

"Thanks for stopping. We got stranded. Well, to be more exact, my friend here doesn't feel comfortable riding his bike down those rocks," one of the two teenagers pointed down the steep and rocky-looking trail, while the other lit a cigarette.

"I hope you guys don't mind," he said, "I really need a smoke." Mo said we didn't mind as long as he could bum a smoke off of him.

Everybody got very comfortable with each other quickly, and we tried to find a solution to their problem together as a group. It became apparent that one of the two motorcyclists was more experienced at navigating off-road terrain, while the second biker, the one who needed to take the smoke break, didn't feel as confident in handling this kind of a challenge.

"I can't go down there—no way!" the second teen said. Mo put his hand on the kid's shoulder to put him at ease and said, "Hey man, don't worry about it. If I take your bike all the way down to the bottom of this hill, you should be able to ride her back out of the bush. This is the worst part. There is no other steep incline like this. Besides, you got your bike all the way up here, bro. What do you guys think?"

There was a brief silence, and then Abu said, "That's a great idea. Hey kid, why don't you take a seat in the back? I will drive the truck. Let's get moving, guys."

What an amazing night. To my surprise I was fully alert and ready to help. My clothes were already muddy and soaked. There was mud in my hair, but at that point it didn't bother me. Instead, I felt supremely alive. There were no technological distractions, and nobody was stressed about getting somewhere anytime soon. We were just a group of people trying to help some kids who got stranded in the middle of nowhere.

Once Mo kick-started the kid's bike, we got ready to follow the two motorcyclists down that steep hill. As we began our descent, I noticed that Mo didn't look as comfortable as we had hoped. He started out strong, climbing the first few boulders quite confidently. But as the path sharply declined, his handling of the bike got shakier and shakier. Soon Mo came to a standstill and waited for us to pull up alongside him. The second motorcyclist waited for further instructions about five yards ahead of us.

Mo's voice sounded far less confident now than before, "I'm not sure that I'll be able to take this bike all the way down the hill. It feels a little heavy for me and doesn't handle too well. All of us could just follow the kid to the bottom of the hill in our SUV. Then those two can ride out back home together on one bike."

Mo took a short breather, looked at us briefly, but before anybody was able to answer he continued in an instant: "Maybe sometime tomorrow, when it's not so dark, they can send somebody who can help out with this clunky bike and get it back down that hill."

Mo was trying to hide his embarrassment, but it was written all over his face.

"Yes, sure," Abu was ready to call it a night. "That sounds much safer, too. I don't want you to crash and then we will have to pay for his motorcycle, but maybe that was the kid's plan all along."

All of us turned to face the kid, who sat squashed behind the driver's seat. Almost on cue, we all started laughing. Although it was pitch black, I could feel a sigh of relief from the backseat.

"I agree, let's get the guys back down safely. Do you know somebody with a pickup or flatbed truck?" I asked the kid.

"Oh, my uncle could help us, for sure. He always tows people around our village and wouldn't mind," the kid responded quickly.

After we arrived safely back at the bottom of the hill, I watched the two take off on one bike, both waving at us. We had a long day. Finally, the three of us were alone again. Abu started stretching out in the back and fell sound asleep at an instant. Mo, seemingly relieved, was focused on the road. I pushed my seat back to stare at the starry sky, wishing that I could extend my stay into next year.

# 9

# Security Patrol Hiccup

I only had a couple of days left in Kamakwie before we were going to head back to the buzzing capital city of Freetown. Sadly, my trip was coming to an end, and there was nothing I could do to change that. The next day, we decided to take one last trip to the Wesleyan School just to double-check that we didn't miss anything. We met up with the school representatives to make sure that everybody involved had their to-do list in order. Then we would go back to the house to pack and head back to Freetown the following day.

*Wesleyan School representatives discussing responsibilities for the*
*GenHybrid lab and curriculum integration*

The meeting went very well, and it appeared that there had already been a lot of hype generated by the upcoming school upgrade. Pastor Daniel blessed the meeting and let us know that there would be a community luncheon held at the center next to the church. Everybody was invited, and we were happy to accept the invitation. The day went by in a flash.

Late in the afternoon Abu, Mo, and I told the group that we had to go back and to start packing for our long journey back to Freetown the very next day. I had lost track of the days and even weeks and had to consult a calendar to realize that it we were leaving on Tuesday and my flight was scheduled for the following Monday. I could feel the wanderlust coming back, knowing that this wonderful place was always going to have a special place in my heart.

The school administrators agreed that we should rest and leave as early as possible in the morning to avoid the daytime heat. I had my "grocery list," as they called it, confirmed during our meeting. All the other players involved knew what to do, and we had a rough timeline that included milestones. In short, once the laboratory was ready to open its doors in January of the following year, classes were to start and the GenHybrid System was going to be integrated.

On our way back, we agreed that the trip to Kamakwie went as planned. We also promised ourselves that on our next visit to Kamakwie the following year, we were going to make sure to spend at least a couple days at the Outamba-Kilimi National Park. I tried not to get too far ahead of myself, but I let the guys know that it would be fantastic to stay at the campgrounds and have a cookout next time we visited the Park. The response I received was a loud cheer, high-fives all around, which I took as a firm "yes."

After packing my belongings, I walked downstairs to pick up a few buckets of shower and toilet-flushing water. In retrospect, the "bucket system" was not the worst thing in the world. In some parts of the Caribbean, electricity and water stop working at certain times and people have reservoirs and generators in place. The same goes for Central America and other parts of the world. It occurred to me that Westerners have gotten used to living in luxury, but this is not how it is for most people on Earth. Granted, I was looking forward to taking a real shower again in a real hotel in Freetown. But for now, I was going to enjoy every minute of rural West Africa.

The next morning Abu started knocking on our doors at around 5:00 a.m.: "Get up. Everybody rise and shine and get ready. We are heading out in about 30 minutes."

I had never been much of a morning person. During my college years I started gradually becoming more of an early riser, but it never really stuck. The transition wasn't the problem. I just naturally gravitated toward working at night and staying up late. Living largely in metropolitan areas, I surrounded myself with likeminded individuals who accepted me for the night owl I was.

Abu's loud knocking wasn't unexpected, but it still forced me to start my day sleepwalking. Needless to say, I wasn't in a mood to be the most joyful traveling companion, but after hearing that our breakfast place opened early for coffee, I felt a sigh of relief. As we walked into the restaurant, we were greeted by the staff and a firm handshake from the owner. Word must have traveled fast, and I was reminded of the encounter with Ibrahim and Adan.

The local people of Kamakwie showed a lot of appreciation for any kind of assistance. It was then that I noticed a birthday cake sitting on the table. There also were a couple of bottles of champagne, tastefully wrapped presents, and plenty of decorations to make for a celebratory day. It was Adama's birthday, and she wanted to share it with us before our departure.

*Adama's birthday celebration before our departure from Kamakwie*

We stayed as long as possible but were painfully aware of the fact that we also needed to beat the heat on our way back down south toward Freetown. After our regular morning breakfast and a good cup of coffee, Adama, her daughter, staff, and family friends walked us out to say their goodbyes. It was a great sendoff, and everybody told us that they would be anticipating our return the following year. Their openness impressed me. Adama's family stayed in touch with me over the years and from time to time sent pictures of their daughter getting married and other updates.

Just as we were taking our seats in the truck, Mo let me know that there was a good reason why his people were known as the "Sweet Salone." "In Krio, our main language, Salone means Sierra Leone, and Sweet Salone is like a nickname for my people. You know, because we are so sweet."

Both of my sidekicks started laughing out loud. The sun was heating up, and I started rummaging frantically through my bags to find my sunglasses. As we were waving our goodbyes, I was more than ready to hit the road and maybe even catch up on a little rest while heading back to where it all started.

The lack of sleep and influx of caffeine was starting to show. I was jittery. It had been a long trip, and we were looking forward to a little downtime. We drove by familiar-looking towns and places that I was fortunate enough to have visited. Just as I started to doze off, one of the frequently encountered police checkpoints stopped us.

Those roadblocks, seen all over the country, were established to create a feeling of safety and security for local people. Over time, the purpose had shifted to generating a side income for police officers willing to patrol checkpoints. Monetary gain in impoverished countries could be challenging, and new opportunities had to be taken. In this case, of course, it would come at my expense.

As the police officer in charge approached our vehicle, he asked for the appropriate paperwork, which meant Mo's driver's license, car insurance, and my passport with a valid travel visa. As Mo pulled out his driver's license and car insurance card, I started searching for my paperwork in my travel bag in the back of the truck. Abu, sitting in the back, hastily raised his arm and started explaining that naturally I didn't carry my passport around for fear of losing it.

It was clear to me then that I needed to follow their lead and remain calm and collected, if I didn't want to be the victim of a shakedown. The police officer in charge took the driver's license and insurance card from Mo and then walked around the vehicle to give it an inspection. The other two police officers were standing by the side of the road awaiting instructions. A few minutes went by before the lead inspector returned. He walked up to the Mo's window and handed over the license and insurance card. Then he said that he still needed to see a valid visa for my stay in Sierra Leone.

As soon as he disclosed his real intentions, Abu decided to exit the truck and to approach the officer in charge. Tensions were rising. It was unclear how the officer was going to react to being approached by Abu so abruptly. To my surprise, the lead officer started to walk away toward his two assisting policemen. The group started gathering in front of the truck to discuss the matter. Abu profusely and openly disagreed with whatever the three policemen had to say.

His temper seemed to be rising with every comment made, to the point where the lead officer asked him to gain composure: "Sir, please calm down," I heard the policeman say, while keeping an outstretched arm pointed in his general direction. The vigorous discussion was going on for a long time, and I started to wonder what the outcome was going to be.

"Mo, how do these things usually end?" I asked.

"Ahm, most people just pay them. I don't think Abu is willing to do that though," Mo replied with a smirk as he looked back at the developing scene.

"Yes, it looks that way. Worst-case scenario, do they have the power to arrest us here?" I asked.

"They could, but they won't. They are only trying to shake us down. Don't worry," Mo said confidently.

"You know, I'm not too worried, but I am very tired and don't feel like taking my nap inside a jail cell."

With that, both of us started laughing, which infuriated Abu even more. Looking back, the scene was quite funny and reminded me of something out of the movies. All three police officers were unwilling to take charge as they tried to calm down an increasingly animated Abu.

Something needed to be done. I feared that the escalating argument might turn violent, and this was something I wasn't going to take a chance on.

"Hey, Mo, let's see if I can get my passport from the backseat. At this point it might just be a matter of them winning the argument. What do you think?"

"Good idea!" he shouted.

I could see that Mo was starting to get uncomfortable, too. I climbed in the backseat, pulled out my passport, and double-checked to make sure I had the visa stamp open on the right page when handing it over to the officer in charge.

"Here is my passport and visa stamp. I forgot that it was in my bag all along."

With an outstretched hand I waved at the officer to come and look. The lead officer came without hesitation, took a quick look, and immediately handed the passport back to me.

"Thank you, kindly Dear Sir. You are free to go," he said at an instant while looking at Abu.

But it became apparent that a disgruntled Abu was not willing to let this go. That day, I experienced firsthand the everyday challenges of local Sierra Leoneans, and their resentment toward corrupt officials was apparent. Once again, Mo and I exchanged glances of uncertainty, at which point another official-looking car without plates arrived.

An exceedingly tall police officer exited the car. He looked and carried himself like a true superior would. He was about 10 to 15 years older than the other three cops, a slim but well-proportioned frame, short grey hair, and well-dressed. His ride-along passenger was a female police officer, who looked like a no-nonsense kind of person.

Now I was starting to feel like this whole thing could go sideways in an instant. The three cops at the scene saluted the newly arrived (as I would later learn) detective. The taller, more experienced policeman turned his full attention to Abu.

"What seems to be the problem here officers?" he said.

Abu was about to explain his story, but the detective cut him off, reprimanding him that he came to talk to his officers. It was made clear to everybody, including Abu, that this matter was going to be resolved *his* way. After the lead officer explained in short sentences what had transpired, the detective exchanged short glances with the female detective, who came over to our truck.

"Would you be so kind to show me your passport and visa one more time, Sir?"

This was obviously not a question but a request. I felt compelled to produce the documentation one more time out of the bag in the back of the truck.

My annoyance level rose. She took a quick look inside the booklet before handing it over to her superior. The tall detective inspected the visa stamp thoroughly before directing his attention to me.

"Good afternoon, Sir," he said casually. "I hope you had a good visit to our country over the past few weeks. Are you planning on visiting other West African nations?" he asked.

"Yes, I had a great stay, and my return flight back to the United States is booked for Monday at 8:00 a.m." My answer was short and precise.

"I see. Today is Wednesday. Where were you and your two friends driving to just now when you got pulled over?" the detective probed.

"Back to Freetown," I said.

"I see," he replied, "Okay, I will hold on to this passport for the time being, but if everything checks out, you can pick it up again at the Youyi Building in Freetown by tomorrow afternoon." With those words he and my passport vanished. Abu got back into the truck, and we took off once again.

# 10

# The Last Stretch

Everybody was quiet for the first few miles, as we fled the "scene of crime," except nobody knew exactly what crime we had committed. Finally, Abu decided to break the uncomfortable silence. Leaning forward, his glowing hot head appeared as he started nodding: "That was really something, wasn't it?" Of course, everybody understood that the question was purely rhetorical. As nobody felt compelled to respond, he continued without missing a beat: "Wow, I mean, wow. Can you believe those guys? I don't think I have ever had roadblock guys be such assholes. This was just crazy."

As nobody was quite ready yet to comment on that mess that we just got out of, Abu was happy to continue to elaborate on his side of the story: "Yes, so, whenever somebody gets pulled over by those assholes," he stuck his head out of the window to shout out that last part of his sentence, "we get off usually quite easily. At times we pay them a couple of bucks, but most of the time after going back and forth we're on our way again."

I couldn't help but wonder why on earth Abu was still so perturbed. I was relieved things didn't get worse, but I was still annoyed.

"Hey, Mo, is this how roadblocks are supposed to go here?" I asked.

"Ahm, well, we got off easy, right? I mean, I didn't have any cash on me or anything. So, yeah, not too bad, I suppose."

It was obvious that Mo didn't want to rock the boat any more than necessary.

"Well, I for one was under the impression that the checkpoint stop would be resolved quickly. What do you think?" I pointed at Mo, who continuously stared ahead at the road, so I continued, "and then suddenly it wasn't resolved. A squad car came to relieve me of my passport. Only this time I didn't get it back."

I could feel my temper rising and had to control myself.

"Why didn't you just come back to truck after the issue was cleared up? What possessed you to continue to argue with those cops?"

I felt like Abu owed us some kind of explanation for his seemingly irrational outburst.

"You didn't grow up here, and you don't understand what we must endure. I have never agreed with the measure of corruption this country has been subjected to for so many years. Can you imagine what it feels like as a little kid to walk to school in the morning not knowing if your parents will be still home once you get back?" There was a slight pause, "No, of course not," Abu picked up where he left off again. "Unless you lived here, there is really no way of knowing, is there? But either way, I do agree that you could have stopped arguing with the guys after he returned the paperwork. Now we have bigger problems to worry about."

I started tuning them out as they continued to bicker for a while longer. My main concern was not to miss my return flight. Time was running out, and I only had a couple of days left to pick up my passport and to get myself cleared for travel. The Sierra Leonean government required a second COVID-19 test before leaving the country. This was to ensure that anybody departing Sierra Leone was COVID-19-free, which prevented international finger pointing.

My gut feeling told me to make sure to get the test immediately after returning to Freetown, which was on a Wednesday. Of course, I also had to head over to that government building now to get my passport back. Admittedly, I was a little nervous about that whole thing. There was just no telling what was going to happen once I entered that building. Chances were that I was going to have to "grease the wheels" to get them to return my passport. Paying people off was just another part of doing business here. It didn't bother me to contribute to the economy in this way, so long as they were willing to hold up their end of the bargain, namely, handing me back my travel documents.

I was deep in thought when I noticed that it had gotten very quiet in the truck. The bickering had stopped, and both of my travel companions had fallen silent. To break the uncomfortable silence, I decided to ask an obvious question: "How much longer do we have to go till we reach Freetown?"

Abu just shot me a long side stare and shook his head. Mo decided not to react at all. So, I kept on pressing. "Hey guys, you know that I still have a lot of stuff to take care of in the next couple of days and can't afford to miss another day."

"Yes, first of all you have to get your passport back," Mo said while looking in the rearview mirror at Abu.

I started laughing. Now that I had a little time to reflect, it really was funny.

"Wow, Abu, you really know how to argue. I mean, seeing your face and hearing you yell. I think that cop might have really been scared for his life," I said.

Mo immediately fell out laughing, "Yeah man, your face was starting to swell up and you just totally lost your shit. I was kinda getting scared myself there for a minute."

Both of us turned around to get a look at Abu's sullen face. Mo started shaking with laughter, and consequently had to pull over for fear of getting into an accident. Abu wanted to get upset with Mo for stopping, but instead he decided to join in on the fun.

"Yes, guys, keep on laughing at my expense. You know I will get you back," he said with a big smile on his face.

"Hey, I have a joke for you, Chris. This will help you understand how we operate here in Sierra Leone," Mo said, trying to catch his breath.

"Great, let's hear it," I was just happy that we were finally on speaking terms again.

"Okay, so here it goes: A priest was driving home on his motorcycle one night, and he was pulled over by a policeman. The policeman asks for the priest's license and then carefully inspects the entire motorcycle with a keen eye for any possible violation. Time went past and the policeman was frustrated because he couldn't find any reason to pressure the priest for money. Finally, the policeman said, 'Father, it's getting late, and it's dark. Aren't you afraid to be driving alone at night?' The priest responded, 'There's no reason to be afraid—I'm not traveling alone. I travel with the Father, Son and Holy Spirit. And the policeman said, 'Well in that case, I'll have to charge you for overloading your vehicle.'"

I heard a shriek coming from the back. Abu was cracking up.

"I gotta remember that joke," Abu said. "You know, I really think that this is how our beloved civil servants go about carrying out their daily duties over here."

Mo was still in a joyful mood but started shaking his head.

"Yes, that really clarified things for me Mo," I said jokingly patting him on the back a couple of times. "Let's get back home now."

In sync, Mo and Abu noted that I had just referred to Freetown as home.

On the remaining stretch to Freetown, we decided to forget about our problems. Instead, we reflected on the fun we had in the northern part of Sierra Leone and the progress made at the Wesleyan Secondary School in Kamakwie. It was good to see my friends share my excitement and enthusiasm for the GenHybrid project and talk about future growth and all the possibilities that came with hybrid learning at a young age.

*Me, Mo, and Abu on our way back to Freetown from Kamakwie*

By the time we got closer to Freetown, it was already getting late. We decided to drop Abu off first. His wife and kids had been impatiently waiting for his arrival. As we got closer to his residence, it became clear that Abu enjoyed living outside of the city center. Driving past the hills that were leading into town, Mo pointed out that there was another national park, the Western Area Peninsula National Park, nearby. As he was explaining the significance of the reserve, I realized that there was so much more to discover.

On my next trip to Salone I was going to make sure to spend more time exploring the outdoors. Abu's house sat on a beautiful hill on the outskirts of town. I was impressed with the care people living in area put into keeping their front yards clean and up-to-date. Abu said that his neighbors get together on weekends to work on the hillside facing the main street to plant trees, place potted plants, and to do exterior masonry paintings to beautify the scenery.

As we arrived at Abu's house, it became clear that locals not only take pride in their environment but also enjoy true community. The entire neighborhood stood outside to welcome Abu back home. His wife and kids didn't leave his side until Mo and I were finally ready to take off to find my accommodations. I really needed a hot shower before bed.

*Freetown neighborhood pride*

After a little driving around, we decided to make a stop at Lumley Beach. I wanted to head further South toward River No 2 Beach, but both of us were getting tired and decided to take a drive down the coast in the next couple of days. All the hotels seemed up-to-date and ready to accommodate. After looking at a handful of options, I decided to go with a medium-priced but very comfortable-looking place.

It was amusing to see the expression on the people's faces as they saw us enter their establishment. The front desk clerk at the hotel that I finally decided to book asked me if I needed to get my laundry done as well. The older gentleman's question was a sign that it was time to call it a day.

Mo shot me one of his by-now familiar full-toothed smiles as he left, "Tenki tenki I padi," he shouted, "I will pick you up again tomorrow." Here he paused for a second, "late in the afternoon." With that, he was gone.

I was so grateful to have been on this wonderful trip, but I was dead tired. After formalities were completed, the clerk handed over my keys, and I went upstairs to my room at once. I fell asleep immediately after my shower.

When I woke up the next day, it was nearly noon, and I was sure that I had missed breakfast. Nevertheless, my long walk around the hotel took me to a foyer that led to the dining room. The staff was still busy cleaning and bussing tables, so I decided to ask the person behind the counter if it was possible to still get something to eat this late in the day. She fixed me a plate on the spot that included a variety of fruit, eggs, bacon, and toast, as well as a strong cup of coffee.

As I was just about to finish my breakfast, I received a text message from Mo. He let me know that he was parked right outside of the hotel, ready to take me to a medical facility in town. Of course, he remembered that I needed to get my required COVID-19 test before being able to leave the country.

Back in the passenger seat I let him know that getting some much-needed rest from that strenuous trip was a blessing. Mo agreed and added that if time permitted, we could still make the trip down the Freetown coastline.

"No 2 Beach is really something special. You need to see that before heading back home," he said, piquing my curiosity.

"Sure thing. Let's just make sure to get my test results back today, and then I still need to head over to the government building to pick up my passport. Maybe we could take care of that on Friday. What do you think?"

"Yes, I will make some phone calls and see if my old high-school buddy still works there," Mo said.

"Really? That would be fantastic, Mo!" I couldn't believe that this might actually work within my tight timeframe.

"Actually, I think he still works there because his sister, who is a friend of my wife, told me that she needed some paperwork signed a while back, and he was able to take care of that for her. I tell you what, when you are inside talking to the medical staff, I will start making calls. Maybe I can make an appointment for us for tomorrow. That would save a lot of time."

"You are truly a lifesaver, Mo," I said.

This turn of events was reassuring and made me feel optimistic. Normally I dread walking into medical facilities. There was an ongoing joke in Las Vegas that posed the question of where locals go to seek good healthcare. The answer was McCarran Airport, meaning if you wanted good healthcare, you should leave town.

As we arrived at the medical facility, Mo was ready to charge in through the front door with the goal of finding "a useful person in a white cloak" that could hopefully point us in the right direction. To be quite upfront, I was neither at ease nor used to having somebody run around taking care of me, but it was good to know that Mo was in my corner.

And then, of course, there was his very efficient way of going about dealing with the local staff. It seemed as if he was not posing any questions, just offering suggestions of how to work me into their busy schedule, and then on how to get me checked out again within an "appropriate" timeframe. It also became clear that Mo already had an "appropriate timeframe" in mind that he was vigorously trying to get enforced. Looking back, if it wasn't for my newfound friends, I might not have reached my goal of getting the GenHybrid Systems building and computer lab constructed in the first place, eventually becoming a vital part of the Wesleyan Secondary School.

Judging from the intensity with which Mo was wheeling and dealing with the medical staff, the language barrier alone might have caused me to miss my flight back. As one of the nurses started walking up to me in the waiting area, I thought Mo had used humor to coax the young lady into attending to my needs.

"Dear Sir," the young nurse said with a wide smile on her face, "Would you be so kind to follow me to the back room?"

"Yes, of course. Thanks for helping us out by the way," I let her know that she was appreciated.

"Well, your friend here didn't give us much of a choice, I'm afraid," again, she flashed me one of those wide smiles and added that they should have me tested within the next hour or so. As I was sitting in the doctor's office, I started to wonder what Mo might have told those nurses to get me moved up the waiting list so quickly.

Finally, the doctor arrived. He seemed very young to be a doctor but turned out to be extremely professional.

"So, you are required to take your COVID-19 exit test," he said in a surprisingly deep voice.

"Yes," I answered.

"Okay, I know these are trying times. But before we get started, I wanted to commend you for your contribution to our education system," he said, while placing his right hand calmly on my shoulder. This made me realize what tactics Mo had really used to get me into the office in a hurry."

"Yes, of course. I am looking forward to getting this project up and running within the next six months. We are all very excited, and hopefully the outcome will be a huge success."

"Oh, I have no doubt that it will be. In my eyes it is already a huge success. It doesn't happen often that volunteers come here to donate their time and decide to fund a project. All of us here wanted to let you know how much you are appreciated," he said while slowly making a half-circle with his free hand to indicate his entire staff.

"Oh, in that case, you should let me pass the test," I joked.

Being the center of attention has never really been my cup of tea, but the doctor started laughing.

"It has been already a great pleasure to get to know you, Mr. Gardner. I'm sure that you will be able to pass this test with flying colors." Again, he started laughing. "Let's get this show on the road, shall we?" he said as he began swabbing my nose.

Truthfully, the swab was taken quite quickly, but I'm not sure if there was actually a rule for how long a swab is supposed to last.

"And that is all there is to it, Mr. Gardner. You are free to go. Please make sure to come back tomorrow to pick up your certificate. You will need that to travel. I wish you best of luck in your future endeavors, Dear Sir"—these were the doc's heartfelt words as he left the room.

Mo was standing in the parking lot, phone in hand, as he wildly gesticulated. Once he saw me, he opened the door and started the truck. Without losing any time, he zipped out of the lot straight into heavy traffic. The main road was congested with hundreds of motorcycles and poda-poda's, the Sierra Leonean version of a bush taxi.

Driving in West Africa most certainly takes some getting used to, but on that particular day Mo was beating everyone. To this day I'm not really sure how we made it past that first four-way intersection without getting hit by a poda-poda, but, somehow, he managed to avoid multiple head-on collisions. Finally, we turned into a more secluded neighborhood. Somehow, we escaped the mess unscathed, and I still wasn't sure what the urgency was all about.

"Mo, have you lost your mind? Why are you driving like a maniac?" I didn't want to interrupt his concentration earlier for fear of causing an accident, but now I was ready to confront him.

"I know, that was crazy, but we need to get to the government building before they close. My friend, the one I had told you about yesterday, just let me know that he is working today, but will be off tomorrow."

This was certainly a turn of events. Mo was in the zone. Come hell or high water, he was going to get us to the downtown Youyi Building before closing time. Apparently, his friend had already scheduled an appointment for us. Mo hastily explained that all we had to do was get there on time.

We were cutting it close. Finding parking was another obstacle to overcome. We managed to squeeze our truck in a parking space that may not have been completely legal. Without closing the doors, we rushed to the main entrance and pushed our way inside before the security doorman locked the gates for the day. Mo urged me to follow him to the second floor. As we walked into one of the many office doors, a man in uniform got up from behind his desk to give Mo a hearty embrace.

"Kushe Mo. How's your family?"

"Adu Adam. Den dey do fyn oo. We tell God tenky," Mo answered in Krio. Loosely translated it meant that they were doing well and that everybody was thankful for that. After exchanging more casual small talk in Krio, both directed their attention to me.

"We will have to make our way to the third floor to fill out some paperwork," Mo's friend said. "My name is Adam, and I will help you to get your travel documents back."

The exchange was brief but courteous. We shook hands and started to make our way up one more flight of stairs. It was apparent that Adam was the person in charge. We entered the "Operation" room on the third floor, and my passport was immediately produced by the station manager responsible for their archiving and documentation system.

"What a relief!" I exclaimed. "Your help with this is very much appreciated, Adam," I added with a feeling of great happiness.

"Don't mention it," Adam said, "Any friend of Mo's is a friend of mine. Besides, this opportunity gave us a chance to finally catch up. It is so hard to get a hold of this rascal." Both men started laughing and shaking hands. "If I ever make it to Las Vegas, you can repay me by showing me around the Strip."

With that I shook his outstretched hand, and we said our goodbyes. Mo and I were relieved and decided to take the elevator down instead of the stairs.

On our way back to my hotel, we agreed to meet up early the next day. It was apparent that Mo wanted me to see No 2 Beach before leaving his beautiful country. The plan was to stop by the medical facility to pick up my certificate as early as possible. We agreed that it would make a lot of sense to get there well before opening hours just in case there was going to be a queue of people waiting outside of the building to be let in. Assuming that the results were going to come back negative, and I wasn't going to have to retake the test, we would be off for a long day at the beach.

Finally, back at my hotel room, I decided to go across the street to get some dinner at the kebab place. The place was lively, and I decided to have a local Star beer. The lager was really good, and the place had great vibes. So, I was determined to strike up conversations with some of the locals. Everybody I spoke to that night had good things to say about No 2 Beach and recommended that I stay at least one night in that area. Apparently, it was going to take a couple of hours to drive to. The beach itself was surrounded by vendors and was known to host festivities all year round.

By 10:00 p.m., we had two tables pushed together and our discussions were getting lively. A young couple, Erika and Larry, from Brighton, England, had decided to join our group as they were also planning to visit No 2 Beach the following day. At the end of the night, we exchanged phone numbers. I wanted to speak with Mo first to see what his plans were for the weekend before committing to a possible meet-up.

The morning after, I awoke to a splitting headache. Our celebrations from the night before had left their mark, but a long shower got me back on my feet in no time. After breakfast I met Mo in the parking lot. On our drive to the clinic to get my test results, I let Mo know about the night before. We briefly discussed the possibility of meeting Erika and Larry at the beach later that day, but we were too preoccupied with the formalities at the medical center to go into it too much.

We arrived at the clinic about 30 minutes before the doors were going to open, but there was already a long line of people wrapping around the building. I was shocked and thought that we might have to spend all day here just to get my results back, which would ruin our weekend plans. As I was expressing my displeasure, Mo calmly looked for a parking spot.

"Hey, luckily we got here early, right?" Mo said while reverse-parking the vehicle.

"Are you for real? Look at that line. What is so lucky about that? We'll be stuck here all day," I complained.

As we were walking toward the long queue of people ahead of us, Mo tugged my sleeve and walked coolly by the line of people, heading straight for the main entrance. I followed his lead. This started to feel like déjà vu. It wasn't much of a surprise that the doors were just about to open, as Mo placed a hand on the window to peek inside the office.

"Hey there," the nurse greeted Mo as she opened the door to let us in, "We have been expecting you. Please just go to the back room, and the doctor will see you in a few minutes."

In my mind, we were going to spend the remainder of the day waiting outside, but instead we were already awaiting my results.

I started to feel guilty about cutting the line and let Mo know about my moral conflict. He simply shrugged it off and answered that this was the way things got done in Salone. If it wasn't for taking charge, people would be left behind and forgotten. Intently looking at me, he let me know that this was a serious matter and that perhaps other places in the world also "respected the squeaky wheel." In those parts of the world it might be a matter of life and death.

On a lighter note, he concluded, as the doctor entered the room, that I should show more gratitude if I had planned on visiting No 2 Beach that day. It appeared that our chatty doc from the day before was in a rush to see other patients. Without hesitation, he gave me my COVID-19-free certificate and excused himself. Mo and I decided not to wait around and within 5 minutes were back on the road again.

*COVID-19 certificate from Freetown*

"So, do you want to just keep on going to the beach, or do we have to go pack for the weekend?" Mo asked.

"Well, I texted Erika and Larry but haven't heard back yet. Let's just drive down the coast and head to the beach. What do you think?" I didn't feel like waiting any longer and was getting excited to finally see what that much-anticipated beach was all about.

"Good call," Mo exclaimed.

We must've been driving for about an hour before we reached the end of a road. The paved road abruptly ended without any street sign to warn us that the off-road part of this trip had begun. It felt a little surreal because the contrast between the road before and after was very extreme. The truck was working overtime to make it past the hills and sand-filled ditches for next 2 hours or so.

Once we arrived at No 2 Beach I was beyond ecstatic. As it turned out, the trip was well worth the struggle. No 2 Beach was truly amazing, and we had a great time visiting and chatting with a variety of street vendors. Venturing further down No 2 Beach, we ran into a market area where we had to pay an entrance fee of $1 in Leones to get in. Most places in Sierra Leone were happy to accept U.S. currency instead of Leones. Nevertheless, it was always a good idea to carry 5 or 10 dollars in 1-dollar bills in the local currency wherever we went. It certainly came in handy on that day.

After trying on a variety of hats, necklaces, bracelets, and many more locally made items, we went on a long stroll down the secluded beach. As it got dark, Erika and Larry still hadn't returned my messages, so we decided to turn around and head back. It had been a long day already, and, truth be told, my African adventure was starting to catch up with me. Maybe a restful night wouldn't hurt, and besides there was always tomorrow.

After breakfast and a good cup of coffee I spent most of my day uploading videos and pictures, for my social media team to use. We had documented the entire trip via Instagram, Facebook, and TikTok. The website genhybridsystems.com was going to give updates on the progress made for the Wesleyan Secondary School computer lab and classroom editions.

*The GenHybrid Systems website served as a platform to promote the initiative*

Throughout the course of my journey, I was sure to keep everybody updated and posted content wherever and whenever possible. In some instances, the Wi-Fi connection wasn't stable enough, and other times the internet was not working, or I just wasn't able to upload for a few days due to time constraints.

I used the last couple of days in Freetown to get my social media content up-to-date and go for long walks exploring the neighborhood. On Sunday afternoon, Mo and Abu came to visit and asked me if I needed a ride to the airport the next day. The Sierra Leone River separated the city from the airport. I was looking forward to the long ferry ride back, which had been a joyride on the way in.

I had a difficult time falling asleep that night. It was hard for me to imagine that I was going to leave this beautiful country, but, of course, I understood that I needed to make my way back eventually. The boat ride was the expected highlight of my return trip. On my way into Freetown, which now seemed like an eternity ago, I saw the vibrant city lights at night as we approached the Port of Freetown. Now, heading back to the government wharf during daytime hours, I was able to strike up a few conversations with fellow travelers. We shared our stories, and one London native immediately wanted to become a sponsor of our upcoming GenHybrid Systems project. Things were looking up, and I was ready to get back home.

# 11

# Final Notes

For the first couple of months after my return, Mo, Abu, and I had chatted via WhatsApp many times throughout the day. I missed them a great deal. We had created a chat group with Pastor Daniel. The Pastor turned out to be a great asset to our cause and was able to assemble a local construction team to get the school renovations underway.

There were many hurdles to be overcome, but within a short amount of time the joint effort started bearing fruit. Once the construction phase had been completed and we were able to get all the wiring in place, the computer lab stations were set up and competent instructors were hired. I was proud to announce that the GenHybrid System's computer lab at the Wesleyan Secondary School in Kamakwie had been given the go-ahead to open its doors. Overall, it ended up being a big undertaking, but once classes started, everybody was glad that the computer lab was finally up and running.

As of today, we are still trying to iron out some of the kinks and improve the quality of classes being taught. One of the biggest challenges was getting the computers shipped to Freetown and then transported to Kamakwie, across the bush, and finally to the northern part of Sierra Leone. Hiring quality instructors proved to be a real test of fortitude as well. But after some trial and error, we finally worked out a curriculum that was manageable for instructors and students alike.

*Wesleyan Secondary School students engaging with GenHybrid Learning Systems on their first day in the lab*

As of today, I am still looking forward to expanding the existing classroom, library, and lab space and to further improving learning for young Sierra Leoneans. I would still love to incorporate other cultures in my GenHybrid learning system. To achieve this goal, I have contacted numerous officials, school leaders, and other officials in positions of power across Asia and Latin America.

I could foresee a bright future for this kind of learning application implemented and utilized not only in countries of need but also across the globe. Young people learning from each other and being able to see and hear each other's experiences and stories will be invaluable to their growth and worldview. It will also benefit future generations. With that in mind, I am hopeful to one day see this plan executed to its fullest potential.